BEYOND THE HORIZON...

travels through consciousness

Marilyn Stacy

Other books by Marilyn Stacy:
  Along the Path
  Dreams...and other altered states of consciousness
  Sometimes You Have to Laugh...a poet's look at cancer

Books may be ordered directly from the author at
www.marilynstacy.com

They are also available at www.amazon.com, www.bn.com
or from www.lulu.com
Search by title or author.

Special thanks to Barbara Blanks for her helpful editorial suggestions and technical assistance in completing this book.

Printed by lulu.com

For Seekers Everywhere

TABLE OF CONTENTS

Introduction

When I began writing this book, I planned to write only about my out-of-body experiences (OBE). Most books I had read on the topic up to this time were similar, in that they detailed each experience the writer had, and they contained nothing about life 'in' body. But I realized that with the OBEs, other extra-sensory occurrences began, or happened with greater frequency. These also influenced my writing.

My first of hundreds of OBEs occurred in 1973, and my unconscious began to manifest itself in other ways. I began to pay attention to my dreams and interpret them. This, in part, was due to my studies in psychology. In the next five or six years I received my bachelor's and master's degrees and learned a lot about dream interpretation.

Also, during this time I became interested in several organizations that combined spiritual and esoteric thinking. Since I tend to be a 'Doubting Thomas,' it was helpful that I always seemed to experience something *before* I read about it. If it were the other way around—if I'd heard or read about something, then experienced it later, I would have wondered if my readings had influenced me.

I began to have lucid dreams, in which I was aware I was dreaming and could change the dream, as well as precognitive dreams (dreams that foretell something). Synchronicities happened with greater frequency. I had several past life experiences that explained some things about my present life. I found lost objects by dowsing, and discovered energy healing. Though I was not expert in any of these things, I found others who were, and who opened my mind to possibilities, especially Marguerite, who was 'there' for me in many of my adventures, and introduced me to many others. My thanks and appreciation go out to her.

These threads of awareness led me to wonder why I had been given the opportunity to explore through my OBE experiences. I'd learned a lot, but to what effect? Was there a point to all this, I wondered? I found there is.

In the last few chapters I write about helping others while out-of-body and teaching others how to do the same. Be sure to read Appendix I, which is a summary of how to go out of body.

ONE

Millions of spiritual creatures
walk the earth, Unseen,
both when we wake
and when we sleep...
Milton, *Paradise Lost*

It was happening again. I had just set my book aside, turned off the bedside lamp, laid my head on the pillow and closed my eyes, when I began to feel lightheaded and dizzy, with a tugging deep inside, as if someone or something was trying to pull me up and out of my body. As I fought against the sensation, I heard the sound of far-away voices calling my name. I was frightened. The only people I'd read about who heard voices were saints or they were insane. I was neither.

I struggled to force my eyes open, then sat up in bed, turned the lamp on, and picked up the book I had been reading. I wanted to distract, to distance myself from whatever it was that had happened, or almost happened. I had been fighting the sensation of falling or being pulled upward for the last couple of nights. That had been bad enough. But voices! I was feeling sleep deprived. For the third night in a row I would be getting to sleep late, and I had to be up early the next day. With my husband, Dean, out of town, there was no one else to get the children off to school in the morning.

I had no idea what the strange, tugging sensations were, or where the voices were coming from. I needed answers. A familiar face and name flickered into my awareness. Marguerite.

I had moved to Dallas with my husband and our five children

in the fall of 1972, and had started taking classes at a community college, something I had wanted to do for a long time. My children bragged to their friends about their "college-student mom," and my husband was always supportive. Marguerite taught one of the college classes I was taking that spring semester. A creative and spiritual woman, she seemed open to any and all ideas. Maybe she could help me; I decided to ask her for advice the following day. Finally, I was able to relax and drift off to sleep.

After class the next day, I described the strange bedtime incidents to Marguerite and asked if she knew what they were and what I could do about them. She said she hadn't had those experiences herself, but did not think I had anything to fear.

"Just surround yourself with white light and let go," she said. "You'll be safe. The light will protect you."

I trusted her, and knew she would never suggest anything that would put me in jeopardy. Besides, I wanted it to be true.

That night, as I turned back the covers, I began to imagine a white light surrounding me. I wasn't sure I was really seeing a light, but telling myself it was there was reassuring. The instant my head hit the pillow, I closed my eyes and heard, "Marilyn, come on." It sounded like a choir of angels, and this time when the tugging sensation began, I took a deep breath, relaxed, and let go. I was instantly pulled up and out of my body, with what felt like gentle suction, then released. I heard, "Good. That's it. Come on."

Instantly, I was flying through the night. My fears dissolved. A soft, cool breeze brushed my skin as I flew through a dark tunnel toward a pinpoint of light that grew larger as I neared it. There were several dark figures in the tunnel, but I flew past them, then burst out into a beautiful nighttime sky lit with hundreds—thousands of stars, a whole galaxy, then another, and another. After a time I noticed several white symbols hanging in the sky. There was a small doorframe, a cross, a circle and a few others I do not remember. They seemed to be four to six feet high from a distance of about fifty yards away. I did not try to move closer. I was puzzled by them, but was so enthralled with the entire flight that I gave little thought to them.

I met several spirits wearing hooded, white robes that obstructed a clear view of their faces. They told me several things that seemed so important I was sure I would never forget any of it, but I did. The second I thought about returning, my consciousness shifted, and I was back in bed. I felt wonderful, and thought I would not be afraid if it happened again. Before that night I had *believed* we are all spirits, and that our bodies are merely temporary residences of our souls, but through that experience I shifted to *knowing* it was true. This flight through a dark tunnel was the first of many journeys filled with lessons and discoveries.

That first night I had no idea what had happened, or how to fit it into my belief system. I had several other 'tunnel' OBEs (out-of-body-experiences) in the next few weeks, then began to experience less dramatic exits from my body. At first they were all spontaneous, but after a time I learned to initiate them myself, and experimented with different modes of leaving. I worked on controlling the direction I wanted to go, and succeeded, at least part of the time.

I walked, or glided, around our house and neighborhood while out of body, flew over and visited cities and countryside on earth, as well as places that are not of this earth. I met other souls on some of these sojourns, and was intrigued with how my five senses operated in those other dimensions.

As anyone who has experienced it can tell you, flying across the country and beyond is exhilarating. The moon and stars provide soft luminance to the nights, and street-lights point out where towns and cities sleep. Sometimes there aren't many people to be seen, and little movement, which can create a beautiful but eerie landscape, a surreal appearance. However, things look different in soft moonlight on deserted streets whether we are in or out of body.

Some nights, if I'm especially tired when I feel a pull toward another dimension, I want to stop the process and just get a good night's sleep. I try to drag myself out of alpha state, that time of deep relaxation in which our brain waves are slower than usual. When I am ready to explore, I focus my awareness just beyond the dimensions of my body, lift up or roll out, then navigate inside the house, outdoors, or into the stars. Lucid dreams can also trigger an out-of-body experience. The variety of destinations is endless, and new facets in this mode of travel continue to surprise me after more than forty years.

Besides a noise that can signal a shift to a different dimension, another indicator is increased vibrations, sometimes subtle, at other times so intense it feels as if someone is bouncing on the bed.

When flying high in the sky, watching bright white stars or shooting stars that glow with color, I can relax on a mentally fabricated swing. At times there are sounds of beautiful music or distant voices. Often 'angel' voices are loud and clear, but they are usually discussing things that do not seem relevant to me. When traveling to other locations, I fly across the earth, sometimes high in the sky, at other times close to the ground, over water, fields, trees and towns, until I decide to land. If I come down into a pond or lake, I can splash through water to land. When I touch the grass and leaves, they feel the same in other dimensions as they do in ours.

I was exploring and learning a lot…but what was this? Why had I never heard of it before?

TWO

Come to the edge, he said.
They said: We are afraid.
Come to edge, he said.
They came. He pushed them...
and they flew. Guillaume Apollinaire

While I found these experiences fascinating, I was still puzzled about them. I tried to find out whether anyone I knew had similar 'unusual dreams,' as I labeled them. But no one admitted to having them.

Months after my first OBE, my brother John, on his way from Boston to Los Angeles, stopped to see us. The night he arrived Dean was out of town. After the children were in bed, John and I stayed up late, talking. When I told him I had been having occurrences in which I seemed to leave my body, he shifted to the edge of his chair and his eyes widened.

"I've been trying to do that myself, using meditation, but so far haven't been successful. How do you do it?" he asked. He told me he had a book with him, written by a man who'd had experiences similar to mine. "You have to read it, but not until you tell me, in detail, everything you can about what happened. I don't want your recollections blurred by what you read."

I was delighted by the synchronicity of John's bringing that particular book with him. He usually carries stacks of books everywhere he goes, but this time he had mailed them ahead. He wanted to reread that one, so he stuck it in his briefcase at the last minute. As I described the events of the past few months, he listened with complete attention, interrupting only to ask a few questions.

I told him about my first tunnel flight and others. I have no loss of consciousness, as when falling asleep, but just before leaving my body, I often hear a loud noise, like a door banging shut, or a buzzing, like an electrical vibration. I feel my awareness shift. Sometimes I float up, bumping the ceiling, and can look down to see my body still in bed. I can push through the ceiling, and walk, jump or fly through walls or closed windows and doors. My hands, arms and legs seem transparent when I'm out in the sky.

"One night I got into bed, closed my eyes, rolled over to my side and stretched out my arm. I felt the smooth wood of the dresser, which was three or four feet from the bed, much farther than I could normally reach. I decided to experiment, and moved my 'spirit' hand down to feel the carpeting, then pushed it through the floor to the cool earth beneath the house."

I told John that if I want to visit a person or place, I fly over cities, fields, woods and rivers toward my destination. "But it's easy to get distracted. When my thoughts stray, I can end up somewhere other than I had intended."

"When you visit out of body, are people aware of your presence?" John asked.

"So far they haven't been, but they often sense that something unusual is occurring. I have communicated with others in different time-space dimensions."

After I told John as much as I could about my out-of-body travels, he opened his briefcase and pulled out a book that put a name to what I had been doing. It was Journeys Out of the Body by Robert Monroe. The author's depiction of his experiences seemed exactly like mine. It was exciting to find that someone else knew about this different reality.

Several years later, when I read Raymond Moody's book, Life After Life, about near-death experiences (NDEs), I was struck by how similar they were to my journeys, even though I am not near death, or even ill. I was not yet aware of others such as Edgar Cayce, the 'sleeping prophet,' who described how the soul leaves the body during sleep, meditation, and other times when we set our consciousness aside.

That night John told me about his efforts to 'astral travel' through meditation. He had become interested in eastern philosophy, religion and the metaphysical when he was a student. We talked for hours about the soul, spiritual beliefs, spirits and reincarnation. We speculated about why it was easy for some to fly off to other dimensions, and difficult or impossible for others, but did not have any answers.

I've thought about it many times since then, and what makes sense to me is this: we all have natural extrasensory abilities and skills that can be developed, but just as with our five senses, some are more finely attuned. Some people have incredible visual acuity, or amazing singing voices, while others have to work to develop their voices, athletic skills, etc. I had learned how to crawl, walk, talk, and understand how *this* world operates, but I was learning how to operate in *other* dimensions now.

At first I didn't see a connection between my spiritual life and the OBEs, which did not fit into my traditional religious beliefs. A Catholic, I had attended parochial schools for twelve years. I know many people remember their childhood God as harsh and punishing, but that seemed unlikely to me. Whether this was a result of what the priests and nuns taught us, or the circumstance of being raised in a loving family, I don't know. It was probably a combination of the two.

I loved the mysticism of Catholicism, the Latin mass and chants, the ritual and drama, and the sense of virtue. We focused on the stories of the New Testament, which emphasize a loving God, and the importance of loving others as ourselves. That made sense, but there were some things I did not understand. The nuns said those things required a "leap of faith." I wondered if they just told themselves to believe or if there was some indecipherable way to leap to faith I was not aware of.

Now, years later, I was stuck in that confusion again as I tried to make sense of my experiences—to understand how they fit into my beliefs about God and the universe. Maybe growing up in Illinois, just across the river from St. Louis, produced some of that Missouri, 'Show-Me-State,' attitude. I could certainly identify with the apostle, 'Doubting Thomas.' I wondered why my astral travels began when they did. It was probably just the right time for personal and spiritual learning.

I found it is easier to find people to communicate with when out of body during daylight hours, but there is less likelihood of being interrupted by telephones or doorbells at night. Eventually I learned time is flexible, so when I 'soul travel' at night, I can often focus on daytime, and find it.

My vision when 'out' is usually good, though sometimes it is slightly clouded, as if through a mist or veil. Generally I don't notice odors, but my senses of hearing and touch are acute, and I love the fresh feel of a breeze when I'm flying. I *am* aware of being in two places at once. This was strange at first, but I soon took it for granted.

Long after my first spontaneous OBEs, I read Carlos Castenada's book, A Separate Reality. Some of his experiences were similar to mine, but of quite a different origin. He used hallucinogenic drugs under the guidance and influence of his teacher, Don Juan. I had no interest in using mind-altering drugs. I do like Castenada's suggestion of reminding yourself to look at your hands when in a dream, which helps you 'wake up' within the dream and begin lucid dreaming, the state in which you are aware you're dreaming and can change the action of the dream.

Yet no matter how real astral travel felt at the time, on later reflection my doubts would resurface. I continually tested myself. One morning, when wide awake, with little danger of drifting off to sleep, I decided to verify to myself that OBEs were not simply a different kind of dream. Closing my eyes, I shifted my consciousness outward and sat up, then lifted out of my body. I leapt through the closed window, glided to the street, then around the block. The only difference in daytime excursions from night-time OBEs was the increased light and activity.

Evidently, spirits, angels and my higher-self find it easier to get my attention in OBEs and dreams than in my everyday, waking life.

THREE

Time and space are modes
by which we think,
not conditions
in which we live.
Albert Einstein

A number of people have asked me if perhaps these experiences are just dreams. Dreams and OBEs are markedly different in one way. I rarely experience a loss of consciousness when going out of body to soul travel or astral travel (which are the same thing), as I do when falling asleep, into a dream. An exception is the lucid dream, a dream in which I'm aware I am dreaming. Lucid dreams seem sharper, more in focus; the colors seem brighter, and when I become aware that I am in a dream, I can sometimes fly out of my body. During these out of body experiences, awareness, or sense of self, is in a location other than my earth body. However, these altered states of consciousness—OBEs, dreams, and lucid dreams—do share a common result: that of illuminating me to what I may not ordinarily understand. And both awaken my relationship with my higher self, fostering spiritual growth.

Dreams can provide guidance and creative inspiration, give warnings with precognitive information, and show us visions of our past lives. When we begin to pay attention to dreams, they may become increasingly vivid, with greater detail. At the same time, we may become more open to synchronicity and intuition, listening and learning in every state of consciousness.

To recall dreams in order to connect with your inner self as a personal growth tool, start by telling yourself at bedtime to have a dream you will remember. Put a pencil and notebook next to the bed and write down whatever comes to mind before you get up in the morning. The words act as a trigger, stimulating further recall of the dream. Write with eyes still closed if you can, to stay in the dream dimension as much as possible. If you get up before writing your dreams, it is less likely you will remember them, because you have already activated your waking consciousness.

My handwriting is hard to decipher even in the best of circumstances, so it takes a bit of work the next day for me to interpret what is on the page. When I write down a dream in the middle of the night, I am often as surprised when I read it later as if it had been written by a total stranger. Sometimes I am so sleepy I convince myself the dream is not important, or that it is *so* important I won't forget it. But I often do. When dreams are confusing we can ask our 'dream guides' for another dream— one that will clarify the first. (Even if you don't know who your dream guides are, you can't see them, and you're not sure they exist, you can still ask).

An example is when Rob, a young client of mine who had many unusual dreams, told me he wanted to be sure he was accurate in his interpretations. I suggested he ask for help clarifying his next dream. When he came in the following week, he was excited. He had an intricate lucid dream filled with symbolism, and during the dream had been thinking that he *probably* knew what it meant, but he was not certain. He heard a loud clear voice say, "Of *course* that's what it means!" Rob told me he woke up laughing. He said, "I guess I told myself!"

Sigmund Freud labeled the 'story' of a dream its manifest content, and the underlying meaning its latent content. A dream is often filled with confusing symbols and puns, but with a little work most of us can interpret a deeper meaning. The earliest dreams we recall may present a life theme or pattern.

Bridges play a part in many of mine, including the first dream I remember, when I was five or six. My brother and I had adopted a turtle we'd found in the back yard, naming him

Tommy. In the dream: *I was crossing a narrow footbridge over the Mississippi River. I could see powerful water surging below as I peered through wide spaces between the wood slats. It was dangerous; some people had fallen through. But Tommy Turtle was with me, and could swim; if I fell, he would save me.*

Crossing a bridge can be symbolic of crossing a barrier, moving from one state of consciousness to another, making an important decision, seeing the other side of things, or making a change; or it can mean a literal crossing over to the other side—death. I am usually adept at crossing the bridges in my dreams, even when there is an element of danger. I feel protected, perhaps because my family gave me a strong sense of being loved as a child. In interpreting universal symbols we must look within ourselves to see if they apply to us.

About the time I started writing this book, I began meeting with several friends to work on the meaning of dreams. We agreed that gaining understanding of a dream has been useful in helping us address unresolved issues. One of the women, Frances, wanted very much to become more positive and forgiving. She'd had a difficult childhood and young adulthood, and at ninety, was eager to 'let go' her anger. She felt that dreamwork might help her do this. In explaining how it works to a friend of hers she said, "We feel it when the right interpretation strikes us. It resonates."

At times, we've had dreams for each other, and when we have questions, we often incubate a dream—ask to dream about something specific.

At Frances' request, I incubated a dream about financial security. In a lucid dream: *I walk down a school hallway, finding money everywhere. It's there for the taking. A lot of people are around, but none of them notice the money. I pick up ten or fifteen stacks of cash. There is always more. As I leave, a woman asks me to stay and help her. I point to the money and say, "It's everywhere. Pick some up."* When I told Frances about this dream, it helped alleviate her fears of the future. She said it reminds her that God always provides and life is abundant.

Everything we need is available if we open our eyes and

reach out. The amount of money we have doesn't determine how secure we feel. People with very little may trust that there will always be sufficient for their needs, while others with high incomes or financial resources often worry about whether they will have enough in the future.

Dreams are a source of information, and if we don't get a message the first time, we may have another, or even a dream trilogy, all about the same thing. Like recurring dreams, they keep coming back until we understand them. They give us information on an ever-deepening level, and may all occur on one night, over several nights—or even weeks. In the following trilogy, my subconscious sent me a message. Because my conscious mind didn't catch on, I was given a second dream to clarify the message, and finally, in a third dream, an even more obvious message.

Dream One. *I was a detective trying to solve a murder, and was driving late at night through a construction area. I ran out of gas. Two friends from my childhood were there. One of them gave me money to make a phone call for help.*

Dream Two. *I was a therapist, with two critical, demanding assistants. I was to see a family with two children. The therapy rooms were messy, but we arranged one so it wasn't too bad. The family's former therapist had died. He had been excellent, and I wondered if I could do as good a job. I could listen.*

Dream Three. *I had forgotten my clothes and was driving home to get dressed. I stopped in front of my house and saw the mailman at the door. I covered myself as much as possible, and ran next door, into their garage. My neighbor let me in and gave me an old robe to put on. I asked her to get my purse and keys out of my car so they wouldn't be stolen.*

These dreams were all about fears—of change, of the future, of being exposed as not good enough, or being inadequately prepared. The dreams show my desire to solve problems, to do a good job, and to safeguard my identity. They underline my uncertainty of the future and that sometimes there is a need to ask for help. The subconscious is a truth detective, discovering and pointing out where we are stuck, which is the first step toward understanding and change. Most of us can identify with typical anxiety dreams, like being late for work or school, forgetting our locker combination, taking a test we are not prepared for, or running from someone or something.

Dream memories inaccessible to the conscious mind sometimes produce feelings of déjà vu, as if we have 'been there' or 'done that.' A few years ago when my husband and I were visiting our son, Robert, in Boulder, he took us into the mountains over-looking the city, to watch a sunset. The view was spectacular, with the sparkling lights of buildings, the moving lights of cars ribboning through the city and the deep blue sky turning peach, pink and purple. Gazing at the glow imbuing the scene below us, I realized I'd seen it before, looking down from the sky in another state of consciousness. Robert told us this was his favorite view, and he often thought of his dad and me when he was there. I think it was the emotional pull that took me there in my dreams.

Dreams can also show us a future event, many times symbolically (a precognitive dream). They can deliver spiritual messages and carry strong emotional impact, helping in ways that are unique to the dreamer. At the time, we immediately get a sense of the meaning of a dream, but on reflection, discover additional meanings, patterns or precognitive information.

***

I took a two-month sabbatical in Vermont. I also planned to retire in three years. After fifteen years as a college counselor and psychology instructor, I was going to open a private practice in marriage and family therapy. I would be able to work with clients without the time constraints of a large institution, and hoped I would also find more time to write.

I attended Breadloaf Writers' Conference in Vermont before going to my brother John's house. Several concerns surfaced that I had not anticipated. A woman at the conference told me a serial killer targeted women out alone at night. "No problem," I said. I had no intention of driving in the mountains by myself at night. In addition, three dangerous felons had recently escaped from a prison a hundred miles north and were thought to be headed south. And there had been a spate of UFO sightings in southern New Hampshire, not far from my brother's house in Vermont. John lived in the mountains, fifteen or twenty miles from the nearest town of a few houses.

My first night alone at John's place, it occurred to me that the basement windows had neither glass nor screens, and no lock on the basement door. The house was wide open to intruders. I began to feel anxious. Then I reminded myself that the nearest small town was about fifteen miles of steep, dirt roads away. It wasn't likely that anyone would bother to come so far from civilization to attack me. I dropped off to sleep, waking late the next morning after a vivid dream about friendly aliens. The serial killer and escaped felons stayed out of my dreams and my life.

But over the next few days I had several other anxiety dreams. In one: *I was walking home from the dentist because I had lost my car keys. The car had been towed, and with it, my briefcase. I called a friend, who said the briefcase was at my office. I found the keys in my pocket.*

In this dream, my identity (lost briefcase) only *seemed* to be missing. I had the power to leave, to take another path, without losing my identity, for I had the keys (answers) all along.

FOUR

Palest blue eyes,
once bright
with sly, secret humor,
now dim, grown enormous,
still cannot contain the sea within.
from *Shades of Transition*

In a dream depicting the fragility of life, and that change is
inevitable: *My family had come to a birthday dinner for me at a*
hotel. It was crowded; I had trouble finding a place to sit near
my parents. The song 'We Live on Borrowed Time' was playing.

The dream described for me the real life situation my
parents were going through. They had been together fifty-six
years, but my dad wasn't doing well. Mom was eight years
younger than his 89 years, but she also struggled with health
problems. My emotions bounced from the serenity of the
forested mountains to anxiety about them.

My brothers and I felt Dad needed to go into a nursing home,
but he refused to consider it. We knew confrontation was inevitable. It came nearly a year later. Mom could no longer take
care of him, even with extra help. Dad finally agreed to go, then
promptly forgot. It was physically and emotionally exhausting
for everyone, not only moving him there, but getting him to stay.
He had tried it, as he said he would, but wanted to go home.
When told he couldn't, he became angry and insistent. He
blamed Mom for everything, and yelled at me. For the first time
in my life I yelled at him.

When his frustration over-whelmed him, he raised his hand

as if to strike me. We were both shocked. As far as I know, Dad had never hit anyone. He dropped his hand and sat down, looking defeated and in despair. Neither of us knew what to do.

I don't remember what we said to each other before a nurse came in to take him to the dining room, but I remember how devastated I felt. As the only daughter, I'd always had a close relationship with him. I hope I said goodbye and that I loved him, but I don't know whether I did or not.

Dad died two months later. His wake and funeral went by in a daze for Mom, who was exhausted, depressed and confused. She needed our help more than ever. We hoped she would begin to feel more like her old self, given time, but she never did. We didn't realize she'd had several small strokes.

Mom's decline blasted me out of the routine of life as nothing ever had, but I found unexpected comfort in writing poetry. My first two poems, about Dad's aging and death, provided an outlet for my intense feelings. My third poem was about a trip to a writers' weekend workshop with a friend. We had driven back and forth on a dark highway in east Texas, looking for a church that was supposed to mark the way. The trip felt like my spiritual path; the map was laid out for me, but I couldn't interpret it, or find my way. The one thing I was certain of is we are all spirits that exist with or without our temporary homes—our bodies. What exists through our five senses is only part of the whole and when our bodies die, we continue on.

My OBEs had transformed 'belief' in life after death to 'knowing.' As hard as the next years were, my spiritual journey intensified. Synchronicities, dreams and family crises led me on branches of my path I never imagined.

About a year after Dad died, my friend Marguerite invited me to a Shalom Retreat weekend at The Farm, a converted church she and a friend bought years before. Surrounded by rolling green hills and trees, overlooking a lake, it was the perfect setting for weekend retreats, meditation, and getting close to nature.

I had been thinking about Marguerite's advice to surround myself with white light, and how it had released the fear holding me back from soul travel. Meeting her at the time I did defines the phrase, "When the student is ready, the teacher appears." She is often present in my life just before I make new discoveries about our inner lives. We might not see each other for months then she pops back into my life just when I'm ready for more stretching. When she called to invite me to the retreat that early autumn day, I said yes, without a second thought. Marguerite's belief that I might benefit from it was enough for me.

The retreat was an illuminating experience, led by a pixie-like woman who used deep breathing techniques and guided imagery to help us work on our emotional and spiritual well-being. For three days we were helped to work on our individual needs, which ranged from resolving grief or anger to spiritual growth. We took turns being the focus of the leader's attention. She guided each of us into deep breathing that helped us shift to an altered state of consciousness, where we could feel and speak from within.

I do not remember what I had initially planned to work on, but at the last minute I changed my mind. I wanted to say good-bye to my dad. It surprised me, but as soon as I said it I knew I needed closure on my grief for my father's death and those last painful months.

Helped by the facilitator to move into deep relaxation, I pictured myself reaching for stars and floating among them. It's difficult to describe exactly what happened next. I didn't see Dad directly, but I had a sense of his presence. I was filled with a warm, loving feeling of connection with his spirit. I thought of how sad we had both been during our last days together and how guilty I had felt for not being as understanding as I could have been. I asked for his forgiveness, and received his answer—that there was nothing to forgive. I said goodbye to him again, this time feeling at peace.

After I finished, the women showered me with love and support. They lifted me over their heads, as we had with each woman in turn, and carried me into the next room, where I listened to the music chosen especially for me by the leader. What gifts I received that weekend.

FIVE

If a man does not keep pace with his companions,
perhaps it is because he hears a different drummer.
Let him step to the music which he hears, however
measured and far away.   Henry David Thoreau

Not long after that retreat I began meeting once a week with several women to discuss our spiritual growth and to share our experiences. Mary was a teacher and an artist. Her Native American mother had struggled to fit into her father's white world. As a child, Mary had been alone a great deal and had been visited by angels often. She views those visits as gifts that helped her survive a difficult childhood. She brought to our group a rich spiritual heritage from her mother's side of the family, with which she had been reconnecting through her art.

At her request, I called to Mary when I was out of body. While her body continued to sleep, I watched as her inner self sat up, turned and smiled. Holding her hand, I flew with her along the fields near the house. We didn't get very high off the ground, about ten or fifteen feet. I suggested we return home and try it another day. Mary had already participated in many Native American spiritual ceremonies and sweat lodges, so she was not surprised when our plan worked. I confess I was.

Another friend, Marianne, was fascinated by my description of astral travel, and asked if I would visit her during an OBE. I said I would try, and a few nights later when I went to bed, closed my eyes, took several deep breaths and visualized myself floating upward. I felt the rapid vibrations that often signal an impending OBE. I had not yet read any of Edgar Cayce's readings about how our spirit 'light body' vibrates at a higher rate, but since the feelings and sounds nearly always signaled the start of a shift to another space-time, I knew what was coming.

I didn't want to fly off into space and overshoot my destination a few blocks away, so I focused on lifting out gently, then stayed close to the ground. I dropped to the street by her apartment building, landing in a skidding, sliding run, which took me a little farther down the block. Moving back with a gliding motion, I spotted her second floor window. I flew up and through the window, landing on the far side of the bedroom, which looked as I had imagined it would. Books, rocks and crystals were everywhere.

Marianne was lying in bed, and as I moved across the room I tried to *think* her awake. She sat up, her eyes still closed. She had some kind of covering on her head. I mentally called to her again and she opened her eyes and looked directly at me. I thought about being home, and was there instantly. The clock on my dresser showed that only a few minutes had passed since I'd gone to bed.

When I talked with Marianne later, she said she had seen someone in the room that night, but not clearly. She had curlers in her hair with a scarf covering them, the 'hat' I had seen her wearing. I knew I had been there in my astral body, but was still puzzled about why I could travel like that.

I struggled to normalize for myself the surprising dimension shifts that kept occurring and hoped to find someone who had similar experiences. When I met a woman who said she had soul traveled many times, I thought we could learn from each other, but she refused to talk about her experiences and what she had learned. She had once belonged to a group in which members used stories in a one-upmanship way, and she did not want that to happen again. It was disappointing. I believe sharing with others should not diminish what we give and receive, but stimulate and enhance growth.

Despite how real my out-of-body travels felt each time, I was still uncertain of their validity. Because so much of what we see during an OBE is different from the reality in our three dimensional world, it can be easy to discount what happens. But later that year I received evidence I could not dispute. A new friend, Elizabeth, was going to Peru for a three week spiritual journey being led by a shaman. She said the group would be small, no more than a dozen women and men, but did not say much more, only that she would tell us about it on her return.

She and I had talked about OBEs. I said I would try to visit her mid-way through her travels, on August 16, my birthday. I didn't think about it again until the night of the seventeenth, but since time and space are relative, I decided to try to find her.

I left my body easily. It was a rainy night, unusual for Dallas in August, and the cool moisture felt good. Soon I was high over the clouds, flying south to try and locate Elizabeth, or for that matter, Peru. A spiritual "direction finder" would have to take me to my destination. I landed in a deep, dark forest, but a few seconds later I caught a glimmer of light ahead. I moved toward it through the trees and reached a clearing. Eight women stood in front of a lodge. Windows covered the front of the building and a wide stone veranda extended across the front. There was one redhead, and at first I thought it was Elizabeth, but the woman was younger and taller. I moved toward them, told them who I was, and said I was looking for Elizabeth. They were excited, saying they'd been expecting me, which surprised me.

The redhead said, "She's inside. I'll go get her."

"I can't stay long. I'm not really in my body," I said.

"That's fine," one of them said. "Neither are we."

About that time someone opened the door to come out, but I felt that familiar tugging and said, "Just tell her Marilyn said hi." Then I was back in Dallas.

I wrote about the experience in as much detail as I could, even drew a picture of the lodge and women, although I'm not much of an artist. When several of us got together on Elizabeth's return to hear about her trip, I asked her to describe where she had stayed on the night in question. Her description was exactly what I had written, including the fact that there were no men on the trip except the guide, who had stayed at a different location that night. All the men who had planned to make the journey had canceled. There were eight women besides Elizabeth, including a tall young redhead.

When Elizabeth read my notes and saw my picture, she said, "Several of the women told me something unusual happened that night. A sort of apparition appeared. It must have been you."

In dreams, prayers, meditations and soul travels, we touch on memory of the universe beyond our present limited life on earth. Those glimpses can drive and motivate our search for knowledge. This added confirmation to my new paradigm of spiritual belief, but I wondered if I would have to prove every new experience to myself.

Since then I've had a number of OBEs that proved, at least to me, that this was a real phenomenon. For a long time I shifted to feeling I needed to somehow prove it to others. I no longer feel that way. For some, there is nothing I could say or do that would 'prove' anything. And that's fine with me. For others, reading validates experiences they have had or gives them a new way to look at psychic experiences.

SIX

REM Flight

Narcoleptic pull toward sleep forces lashes tight,
as distant voices beckon without words.
Powerful sound, a thunderclap
slams shut the door of the known,
propelling through tunneled darkness.
The quickening breeze aids flight
toward distant light that grows ever brighter.
Final burst into an infinity of stars,
unending space, illumines all.
Reaching, soaring closer to the welcoming light,
beginning of awareness flickers.
Abruptly, fear intrudes
and a soul folds back into the shell
that next day denies its journey.

Several out of body experiences I had were interesting, but seemed to have no rhyme or reason. In one of them I 'dropped' onto a long path through a park and began to run with many other people. It was night, but the stars and moon were so bright I could see clearly. I asked a woman, "Is this the way?" She nodded, and as we ran, we talked about the beauty of the sky. After a short time, I was 'pulled' back to my room.

Once I flew through the dark tunnel and stopped at the end, stuck. I couldn't see anything—no light, no sky. I reached my hand through a velvety curtain and felt around, trying to determine what was in front of me. A hand grasped mine and pulled me through. After I was on the other side, I saw bright stars glittering in the sky all around, but there was no one in sight. Who had pulled me through? I thought it might have been one of the spirits or angels who called to me and encouraged me on my first OBE. Spirits are energy, taking bodily form only to help us connect with them, but I am still surprised when I hear a voice or feel the touch of a being I cannot see.

On another night, wanting to explore, I relaxed and concentrated on my breath. As I did, my vibrations intensified. I lifted out and flew high into the sky, feeling calm and at peace. After a time I dropped softly into a clearing. I wondered if I was in the present, past, or future. Stooping down, I dug my fingers into the soil. It felt the same as my garden at home. A small, white frame house stood about twenty yards away in a large bare yard.

Curious, I walked toward it, then hesitated a moment before going up the steps to the narrow porch. Things looked peaceful, and I knew I could shift quickly to present time and place if necessary. I knocked on the door.

An elderly woman opened it. She said something I did not understand, and motioned for me to come inside and follow her through the kitchen to another room. An ordinary looking man was sitting on a sofa, and I sat next to him. The old woman indicated that the man and I were similar. There was something around my waist, like a life preserver. I asked the man if he had one too.

He nodded then asked, "Do you remember any of their normal faces?"

A twinge of fear tugged inside my chest. I wondered what the elderly couple's 'normal' faces were like, and what dimension we were in. His face began to fade. A moment later I was in my own room.

During an OBE later that year, I saw a girl fall from the edge of a cliff. She screamed. I flew down to try to help her, reached out, and she clutched my hand. Her nails were like sharp claws. I told her she was hurting me, but she wouldn't loosen her grip. My only escape seemed to be returning to my body, but I didn't want to respond to fear by running (or flying) away. I called for help from my angel. She was there instantly and helped the girl reach ground safely, leaving me free to explore. I flew through the night, past the lights of cities, over tree-tops then closer to the ground. Drops of rain cooled my face as I landed in a dense forest. I was a man in that time and at that place. Sensing danger, I ran. I heard a noise behind me, turned, and through the mist and fog, saw a dark horse with a white star on its forehead racing toward me. When it was close, I grabbed its mane and jumped on. Racing through the woods, the horse slowed as we entered a small town. Several people greeted me.

I dismounted and led the horse toward an inn, where a young girl leaned out a window. When I motioned to her, she came outside. I asked if she had seen the new house. (I don't know why I asked her this). She nodded and we walked toward it. I was trying to remember who and where I was. I knew I had been there before, that I had a life there. Everything felt familiar. Then a noise startled me and I was back in Dallas.

About this same time, I traveled out-of-body several times to another town different from any I remembered visiting before. I was an ordinary man with an ordinary life. People were friendly when I arrived, asked where I'd been, and said they had missed me. Everyone wore uniform-like clothing and there were few visible signs of modern life—no electric or phone wires, no television antennas. I was aware of my identity when in that universe, but upon returning, could remember very little.

Several years later, I read an article by Robert Monroe, who had OBEs similar to that one. He called them experiences in a parallel universe. Many people believe that we not only have past lives, but also parallel existences in other dimensions. I don't know if we do, but it certainly felt that way at the time.

About a week later, after lurching vibrations, I shot out toward bright, white stars and watched as they transformed to beautiful colors. Then I flew toward the ground. Landing at the edge of a lake, I splashed through it to a muddy shore. Three children in swimsuits, the oldest a girl about twelve, were playing in front of a large house set in the midst of tall trees. I asked if their parents were home.

"Our father is," said the oldest.

"May I see him?" I asked.

"You want to see him, like all the others," she said.

"I'm not like the others. Are any of them from another planet? From outer space?"

"From Alpha?"

"No. Earth." Evidently I was not their first visitor from another planet or dimension.

They led me to the house, which was built of shiny, white stucco-like material and we went inside. The front room had a few small, round tables scattered about; several people mingled there. The children told a man that a woman was there from outer space.

"And what does she look like? An alligator or a reptile?" He was teasing them.

I said, "I don't think so. Do you have a mirror?"

The smallest girl handed me a mirror. I saw the reflection of a younger version of myself, my hair still brown. When I said, "I look like this in my other life," it served as a reminder that I was out-of-body. I felt a pull, then was back home. I considered returning, but was tired and went to sleep instead.

SEVEN

See, I am sending an angel
ahead of you to guard you
along the way. Exodus 23:20

I sometimes wondered how my family fit my paranormal experiences into their belief systems. Then my daughter surprised me with a story she came across while doing research for a Texas/Mexican history class.

Maria de Agreda, who was born in 1602 in Spain, entered a Franciscan convent and became a nun at an early age. She experienced some 500 deep trances in which her body temperature dropped, and she couldn't be aroused from a coma-like deep sleep. On waking, she said her spirit had been transported to a distant land, where she taught the Gospel to pagan people. Maria reported the bilocations to her confessor.

In 1629, a delegation of Jumano Indians from Texas appeared at a Franciscan mission near present-day Albuquerque, exhibiting a rudimentary knowledge of Christian symbols such as the cross. When asked who had taught them, they said, "the woman in blue." Maria always wore traditional Franciscan blue. Two priests accompanied the Jumanos back on the 300-mile trip to the Pecos River. On arrival, the priests were greeted by a huge congregation of Indians, who said the woman in blue told them priests would be arriving and would convert the Indians to Christianity. The priests baptized some of them, but did not set up missions there.

Susan thought I would be interested in hearing about someone else leaving her body. I was, but more important to me was my daughter's matter-of-fact belief in the phenomenon. She said she had known for a long time about the occurrence of mystifying things.

Years earlier she had read that plants respond to human voices. A plant in her apartment was limp and lifeless. She was about to throw it out, but decided to try reviving it by giving it special attention and care. She talked to it encouragingly that evening. The next morning when she went into her living room, she saw that not only had the plant 'greened up,' but a beautiful flower had emerged and blossomed.

It has been said, "For those who believe, no proof is necessary. For those who do not believe, no proof is possible." People who are certain that a non-physical reality does not exist deny almost anything that doesn't fit that belief. During the age of science the past two hundred years, those who disclosed contact with an angel or spiritual being, or told of an OBE or NDE, have been considered mentally ill. Yet we have all experienced altered states of consciousness, when we release our deliberate cognition.

An example is when we participate in a sport while in the 'zone' or the 'flow.' I played basketball in high school, and can still recall the feeling of being in the flow, just letting it happen. During one game it seemed as if I could toss the ball without even looking and it would swish through the hoop. Golfers and tennis players talk about their 'inner game,' when they visualize what they plan to do. When they play, they relax into the no-think zone. When we let go conscious thinking and planning, we allow our inner self to do its thing.

For instance, when driving a car, have you ever gone past where you were headed, then just snapped to? You 'woke up,' even though you weren't asleep. Your cognitive, thinking self was on hold. Or have you ever daydreamed and missed an entire lecture or half a movie? Many people have told me there are times they seem to be looking at themselves from the ceiling or from a corner of the room. The instant they realize it, they snap back into the body.

If an incident was not acceptable to your belief system, more often than not, you forgot it quickly, or discounted it. If you've tried to tell someone about floating out of your body in a near-death-experience, you may have been told that NDEs aren't real. There are differences in what people have reported about them, but are any two experiences exactly alike? Do two people give identical descriptions of a trip or an accident? Why would we expect each person's other-dimensional experiences to be the same?

During other states of consciousness, our brain waves change; measurable shifts can be seen during an EEG. Opening the door to the unseen world of soul travel can bring greater awareness of other psychic phenomena. The more I experienced, accepted and believed, the more doors opened to me. Whether through energy healing, clairvoyance, lucid dreams, OBEs, angel or spirit visits, seeing auras, or other multidimensional incidents, we connect with higher vibratory states when we let go of our willful thinking. This allows better access to the inner self and enhances spiritual growth.

I had many questions about my OBEs, and was curious about a deeper meaning to them. I was experiencing cognitive dissonance, which can occur when new information or experience doesn't fit within our existing framework of beliefs. To erase the uncomfortable feeling of dissonance we can either ignore new information or rethink our established concepts of truth and reality. Learning is a lifelong process. Ideas, information, and knowledge emanate from every level of consciousness. I've received many helpful reminders, suggestions, ideas and solutions in dreams.

For example, in a lucid dream, a dream in which I became aware I was dreaming, I tried to help some young adults, who were dusting furniture in their new house. They were rude and critical. I wondered why I should try to help them when they acted that way then I realized they hadn't asked for my help, nor had I asked if they wanted it. The words I scribbled down in the middle of the night about that dream were, "Wait until asked. I walked back to my side of the fence," which symbolizes a return to this side of consciousness. Dreams that include fences or bridges, or in which we cross roads, the sea, etc., are often metaphors for going back and forth to other dimensions.

The above dream gave me useful information. As a counselor, mother, and caregiver to my aging mother, much of my time was spent helping others. I've learned to not work harder than my clients do, to allow them to discover solutions to problems themselves, so any changes or decisions they make are theirs, not mine. The dream reminds me to wait until asked before jumping in to help solve problems.

In another dream: *I was at my childhood home. There were five TV sets. Dad was talking on the phone to his dentist about TV, jewelry, etc. Dad said he had just retired. I was aware I was dreaming.*

This reminded me to pay attention to the many avenues available for communication, even with those who have passed on. We can also commune with our inner self through altered states of consciousness in dreams or during mediation. The jewelry symbolizes spiritual truths and wisdom of the higher self, or reflection of divine light.

We find universal meaning in dream symbols and metaphors, but it is important to pay attention to what resonates for us as individuals. A dream may mean one thing to me but something very different to another, because of our differing personal histories and belief systems. Although they are not all of equal importance, the more we pay attention to them, the more complex and helpful they become. Dream interpretation is like good literature, with layers of meaning and complexity. Understanding the emotions and symbolism of dreams helps us find their underlying themes or messages.

When changes occur in our lives, we often find there is a shift in our dreams. After we moved Mom to Dallas in 1992, I noticed a stronger spiritual element in my dreams. In many I am walking, running, biking, or driving down a street; all these are about moving along my path. In one of my favorite lucid dreams, my "Red Bird" dream: *I am walking with friends. I see Shirley MacLaine, the actress, writer and director, striding through a crowd toward a railroad embankment-tunnel, followed by a large retinue. We are headed for the same place, but I choose a different path, and am soon alone in the calm, green countryside. I walk in the middle of the road at first, then on one side, where colorful pebbles slow my progress a little, but make the walk more interesting. I come to a fork in the road marked by a majestic old oak tree, and turn to the right, where I'm joined by a large, brilliant, red bird. I tell myself not to frighten it.*

To my surprise, we begin to talk. With its permission, I rest my hand on its back as we walk. The shiny feathers are smooth and strong. I wonder aloud how it has lived long enough to grow so large, how it has avoided being caged or shot, and I ask if it is afraid to be so exposed to view on this road. It assures me there is no danger. "I can fly whenever I wish." Then I remember that I, too, can fly if I choose. I don't know what is at the end of this road, but it is the right path for me.

This dream reminds me that I can fly, at least spiritually. Having explored many beliefs in my search for spiritual truth, I'm aware of following my own path. When I 'gestalt' this dream, looking at each part of the dream as different aspects of myself, I recognize that I do not choose to follow another, nor do I wish to develop a retinue. My shoes may be large, but I can walk in them, using the 'glue' of intent, will, and inner aware-ness. Ultimately we are all headed toward our spiritual home, but enriching as it is to share with others on the path, I must choose my own timing and direction, with all its stumbling blocks and side trips.

When I close my eyes I can still see my dream bird's bright red feathers and feel their smooth firmness. Symbolically, cardinals remind us to renew our vitality and recognize our life roles. Their loud clear whistle tells us to listen to what is 'blowing in the wind,' to listen to our inner voice, and to assert our feminine aspects of creativity and intuition. A dream about cardinals may also reflect past-life connections to the church, reviving traditional religious beliefs.

In a 1998 interview, former astronaut Edgar Mitchell,* who was one of the few men who walked on the moon, said he considered himself an explorer of 'inner' space. He worked on concepts of consciousness. He founded the Institute of Noetic Sciences, which furthers the explorations of the interdisciplinary field of consciousness research, including spiritual, mind-body, ecological and conventional science. He said it is not a religion, and that the "guru approach is not necessarily the best approach." He thought of himself as a seeker and believed each person has his or her own path to follow, saying, "It is a participatory process that we are involved in, an interactive process."

* Mitchell died on February 4, 2016

EIGHT

Two roads diverged in a wood, and I,
I took the one less traveled by,
And that has made all the difference.   Robert Frost

As a rule, I tend toward optimism, but ignoring warning
signals can potentially lead to harm. Precognitive dreams can
ease the shock or pain of an event; in other cases, especially
when we dream about others, there is really nothing we can do.
We don't always recognize or remember the message in dreams,
and the sense of déjà vu we have may be the dim recall of a
dream message.

An example of a dream spelling out information came from a
new friend, Naomi. She told me that years earlier she wanted to
move, and had meditated, visualizing a house and surroundings,
while keeping in mind she wanted a house that did not cost a lot,
but would increase in value after she bought it. She received bits
and pieces of information in her dreams, like parts of a puzzle,
which eventually led her to the house she wanted in a setting just
as she had visualized. The day after she signed the papers, she
learned a new highway was going in not far away. The value of
her property doubled overnight. She had faith in her dreams and
her intuition. If she had ignored the messages she received, she
might still be wishing for, rather than living in, her dream house.

I'm still puzzled about an especially vivid precognitive
dream I had. *I was on a large boat, near Coronado Island (a*
place I had never been) sitting at a table next to a window. I
looked to my right out the window just as a red and yellow boat
surfaced. (It was a submarine) I could have reached out and

41

touched the captain of the boat. He seemed threatening, and I was frightened. There was more to the dream, but it was the brightly colored boat that made a strong impression on me.

Months later, I visited my son and daughter-in-law, Sang, in California. One day Sang suggested we take a boat tour of San Diego Bay. After boarding we climbed to the upper deck and sat at a table to relax. A few minutes after we pulled away from the dock I glanced to my right. I was shocked to see the red and yellow boat from my dream anchored directly across from us. Excited, I pointed it out to Sang, who told me it was docked at Coronado Island." I asked someone about the vessel and was told it was a submarine rescue vessel. I have thought about whether there was a reason for that precognitive dream, but haven't come up with a thing, other than as a reminder to pay attention to my dreams.

In the days immediately preceding September 11, 2001, many people had dreams of planes crashing, buildings burning and people dying but weren't aware of their significance until later. Early that morning I dreamed *a crazed man, driving a huge vehicle, was crashing into others, killing them. Some of us flew through the sky, trying to escape.*

That dream shifted abruptly to a seemingly tranquil scene in which *my daughter was about four. Wearing a pink tutu, she was the picture of innocence. She walked to the street to get the newspaper (which I knew had important news) then she disappeared. I ran after her calling, "Help! Call 911. It's terrorists!"* My cries woke me. I felt the dream meant something terrible was going to happen that would rob us of our childlike innocence. A few hours later I watched on television the destruction in New York, Washington, DC, and Pennsylvania.

Henry David Thoreau wrote, "Our truest life is when we are in our dreams awake." Years ago, in one of the first precognitive dreams I recall, I was given a warning that helped me diminish the emotional consequences of a negative experience that was to occur. I was enrolled in a doctoral program and was taking two courses. One class was a practicum, the other, an advanced theory course. I rearranged my work schedule to allow for the classes twice a week.

In the practicum course we worked with clients in direct counseling and observed each other's therapy sessions to provide feedback. I had been in charge of personal and crisis counseling at the college where I worked for several years, but I looked forward to gaining new information and improving my skills. The sessions were videotaped; it felt awkward being 'on camera' at first, but eventually I got used to it and lost my self-consciousness. Doctoral students in their final year also observed the therapy sessions through a one-way mirror, as did the professor.

The young man I was counseling had serious problems. He told me he had been in therapy several times, but this was the first time he stayed with it. During our time together I helped him decide to end a bad relationship. He was making other changes in his life as well. He felt good about how his therapy was progressing and so did I.

One day at lunch, Cindy, a fellow student, asked me to observe her counseling sessions. She had been criticized harshly by her student-supervisor and was worried. I was surprised she was having problems. She was bright and understood theory well. After watching her in session, I was even more puzzled. She was genuine, caring, and her client was doing well. But at the next group session she received another negative evaluation. We were all expected to give input. I did, and was supportive of her work.

Soon I found myself in the same sinking boat as Cindy. One day my student-supervisor asked me why I didn't 'call' my client on something he said. She said, "Tell him he's lying." I was stunned. I could see no therapeutic benefit in that approach, even if I thought he was lying, which I did not. She said I should tell him anyway, which made no sense to me. I asked questions, trying to understand her reasoning. The bottom line is she wanted me to do something I believed would be detrimental to my client. This was a 'catch-22' if there ever was one. If I agreed, I would have to say things in therapy that I believed were not in my client's best interest. When I disagreed, it 'proved' to her that I was unwilling to follow supervision.

From then on, things went downhill. The classes I had begun with such enthusiasm became a puzzling nightmare. Cindy dropped out of the program, as did several others. Power trips were in full flow on that campus and I was taken completely by surprise. I learned later that others in this program had experienced similar problems in past years.

I had been making A's in my theory class, but now that professor began making personal, critical remarks to me in class, and writing cutting comments on my theory papers that indirectly referred to the practicum class. I had tumbled into a twilight zone of academia. I didn't want to spend the next couple of years in this negative atmosphere, but I did want to finish the semester and work with my client. I had put time, money and energy into the classes and thought I could surely stick out the last weeks and receive those six credit hours. Grading was at least partially subjective, so either or both professors might give me a B, but I could live with that. I would do my best work, try to be as cooperative as possible, finish the semester then leave the program.

With this decision made, much of my inner turmoil dissolved. In both classes I tried to relax and do my best, without taking offense or expressing anger. My theory professor, whose negative treatment toward me had been obvious to some of the other students, seemed surprised at my calm attitude. Before the end of the semester he reverted to his original behavior, treating me as he did everyone else. I was beginning to think I would make it through the fall semester. Then one night I had an extremely vivid dream.

I was riding a bicycle along the bluffs of the Mississippi River, not far from where I grew up. Cindy was riding on the back of my bike. When the path got bumpy, she jumped off. I continued, and came to a wide crevice. I thought I could toss the bike over and jump across, but when I threw the bicycle, it fell short. I could hear it falling down, down, into what seemed like a bottomless pit.

I woke with a start, sat straight up in bed and said aloud, "What makes me think she will even give me a B?" (In graduate school, a grade lower than B is not acceptable as credit toward a degree). My unconscious knew what my waking self didn't want to admit, and was warning me. The dream showed me I was kidding myself (the bluffs) in thinking this was a safe journey. My bike crashing far below me meant things could be even worse than I'd let myself think.

Weeks later, when I received my grade card, with A in theory and C in the practicum class, I was not surprised. My dream had prepared me. I learned that the professor had never observed my counseling—not once. When I asked her about it, she told me it was because of a personal relationship she had with my client. I wondered how she could justify my grade, and protested it in writing, but to no avail.

I did some soul searching after that semester. I did not want to continue in a program I no longer respected. That spring I signed up for a creative writing course and found time to write again. It felt wonderful.

My bicycle dream cushioned the shock when I received that grade, but I held on to my anger and resentment toward the professor. I had forgotten a lesson about forgiveness that I had received six years earlier when a serious injustice had been done to someone I love, with devastating consequences to our family. I had been filled with anger, even hate, and it shocked me to find I was capable of those feelings. I could barely eat or sleep, and felt enveloped by a black cloud of doom. A huge weight seemed to literally be sitting inside my chest. This feeling continued for weeks. One morning I was sitting on our front porch steps. I felt heavy pain and sadness. The weight of the world was crushing my spirit, making every breath difficult to take.

All of a sudden I became aware of what a beautiful day it was. The air was fresh, the sun warm, the birds were singing. I realized my anger was not helping anyone, nor did it change the situation. Holding on to those feelings was only hurting me. I decided to let go, to forgive, and in that instant I felt the weight in my heart physically begin to move up, then out the top of my head. It was gone! I was shocked at the clear, immediate response to my decision to forgive. Nothing else in the world around me had changed, but I felt totally different inside, both emotionally and physically.

As I thought about that day, I tried to release my anger toward the professor. A Zen proverb says when we hold onto anger it is like holding a red hot coal in our hand. We are the only ones being hurt. All we have to do in order to stop the pain is open our hands and release the coal—our anger. I let it go.

Forgiveness produced less dramatic results than it had in the incident six years earlier, but it was a great relief to let my negative feelings go. Moving from intense anger to joy by simply releasing my anger felt like a gift from God. It was a valuable lesson to be shared with family, friends and clients about forgiveness. I can speak from experience. When we forgive, we benefit as much as, or even more than, the recipient of that forgiveness.

Since my 'bicycle dream' I've had a number of precognitive dreams; clients and friends have related dreams to me so clear and specific that when the 'real life' experience occurred, they felt it was like watching a movie they were in and had already seen. In one case, a young woman had repeated dreams about a car accident. One night that accident actually occurred, with all the people and circumstances she had dreamed. Because of the dream's warning she managed to avert some of the potential harm. She never had that dream again. She said rather than frightening her, the experience has made her more thoughtful about recurring or vivid dreams. She sees them in a positive light.

In *Leaves of Grass*, poet Walt Whitman asks if we only learn lessons from those who admire us. He asks if we do not also learn from those who "braced themselves against you, and disputed the passage with you?" We do, but it can be difficult to recognize those lessons and even harder to appreciate them.

NINE

*To find that ye only lived, died and were buried under
the cherry tree in Grandmother's garden does not make thee one
whit better neighbor, citizen, mother or father! But to know that
ye spoke unkindly and suffered for it, and in the present may
correct it by being righteous—that is worthwhile!*   Edgar Cayce

Reincarnation, a fascinating theory, didn't fit my traditional
beliefs nor apply to my life. But my beliefs were changing. Over
two-thirds of earth's people believe our souls return many times,
learning life lessons on the path toward completion. To adher-
ents of Eastern religions such as Buddhism and Hinduism,
reincarnation is a fact. Many books and articles describe children's memories of past lives and verification of those recollections. Writings of great philosophers and thinkers such as
Aristotle, Thoreau, Plato, Schopenhauer, and poets Wordsworth
and Walt Whitman, express belief that the soul survives death
and returns to a new body.

Reading Edgar Cayce's work opened my mind. Cayce, the
sleeping prophet, helped many with his clairvoyant gifts. He
held strong Christian beliefs, without shutting out extrasensory
experiences that seemed antithetical to my own belief system.

A major shift was inevitable after I met Linda W, a minister
and past-life regression specialist, at a spiritual discussion group.
When I asked her help in accessing a past life, she asked why I
was interested. Besides curiosity, I hoped to learn something that
would contribute to my spiritual growth. Linda said that is the
best reason for past-life regression.

A week later I lay on a mat in her living room, covered with a blanket, and we began. A tape of chimes played softly in the background as Linda helped me into a state of relaxation. The temperature in the apartment was moderate, but I immediately began to feel cold. Throughout the session, I kept asking Linda for more and more blankets. I felt like I was floating in a sea of black sky for a long time. Nothing was happening. She asked me to visualize several scenarios such as going through a door, walking in a field, or picking a flower, all designed to help trigger transition to a past life, but I continued floating, hearing her voice as if from a distance, seeing nothing.

At last, far below, a patch of brown appeared that gradually lightened to a deep yellow. Linda asked me to move closer. My vision, like the lens of a camera, zoomed down to ripe wheat fields. At the edge of the field there was a small, white, steepled church with rectangular windows arched at the top. I could not see inside. I shifted my gaze to a winding path in front of the church that sloped down a hill to what seemed like an old Pennsylvania Dutch village. A girl in a long, cotton print dress and apron with a bonnet covering her hair lay face down on the path. She was dead.

Linda asked if I could see who she was. Although I could not see her face, somehow I knew that I had once been this girl.

"Move a little farther back in time. What happened just before this?" Linda's voice floated around me, directed me.

I watched the girl walk down the path to the village. She was ill and needed help. It was very early in the day; no one else was around. She went to the door of one house, stood there for a minute, but did not knock. She turned away, as if she knew there would be no help from anyone in the village, for she was pregnant and was not married. She started back up the path to where I had first seen her.

Then I *was* the girl lying on the path, having painful contractions for what seemed a long time. I was the girl, but I was also *Marilyn*, still connected to Linda's voice. Despite being afraid, I was aware, from the perspective of the present time, that I was not alone. The contractions reminded me of giving birth to my children. They also aroused recollection of how it feels to be born and to die. I began to cry, and although the pain lessened, the contractions were still intense.

"You can ask for help. You're never alone," I (Marilyn) said to the dying girl. As the girl, I said, "It hurts to hold on. I can't stop it. It's happening. No, it can't be."

At that moment, my essence pulled up and out of the body with a sensation somewhat like the separation or release of two magnets. I felt lighter and free. Looking at the girl from above, I said, "She doesn't hurt anymore. It doesn't last. She is there, like old clothes. She did not know the answers." Surprisingly, I felt fine. The girl I had once been was dead, but I still existed as the soul, the essence. I flew higher and higher, leaving the body of the girl behind, and said, "It's far away already."

When Linda asked what I had learned, I repeated, "We are never alone. I can ask for help. Dying and being born is easier than giving birth. I keep learning, then forgetting, doing it over and over."

"What do you keep doing over and over?" Linda asked.

"Being born, giving birth, letting go, trying to remember."

I flew back down toward the wheat fields, which had become a blurry brown/gold again and saw the church, the path, the girl, and the village. "She didn't know it, but she was not alone," I said then I went back, briefly, to the comfort of the dark, before moving into the light.

After awhile, Linda gently told me to come back when I was ready. When I was fully back I was surprised to see how much time had passed. As I began to warm up, I peeled off layers of blankets she had put over me. My feet had been freezing; now they were warm again. I had spent a long time in the 'between lives' stage, but Linda was patient, not making me feel rushed. She gave me the notes she'd taken and we listened to the audiotape she made of the session. She emphasized the importance of thinking about why I experienced this particular past life, rather than another.

"How can this benefit you in what is occurring in your present life?" she asked.

I have thought about her question many times since that day.

I often sink back into doubt after I've learned something through a spiritual experience. I also have a tendency to 'go it alone.' My independent nature at times gets in the way of my personal growth. I need to remember to ask for help, and to have faith in what I experience.

About a week later, during meditation, I decided to try and access another past life, with the intent of learning more about spiritual growth. I began with deep breathing as I focused on my intent, but about the time I felt ready to let go, I became anxious. I said the prayer to my guardian angel I learned as a child. I felt calmer then I flew out-of-body. I was no longer frightened, but I started another prayer: "Hail Mary, full of grace." As I began the next line, "The Lord is with thee," a beautiful male voice joined in the prayer. I said to myself, "That sounds like Jesus," and heard, "It is."

I was amazed and thrilled, and felt protected and loved. Others joined in the prayer, but their voices were fainter, as from a distance. When we finished, I thought about saying the "Our Father," thinking Jesus might continue to pray with me, but I didn't want to be greedy. I was grateful He had come to help. I did not turn to look at Him. Hearing His voice was enough.

I had come out of body for a reason, to return to a past life, and it was time to do so. Flying toward the dark earth below, I saw a door, nearly hidden, like the entrance to a cave. I went in, hoping to be inconspicuous, even invisible. The room was long and narrow. A long table to my left was laden with goblets, wine and food, mostly fruits and bread. Men and women wearing long garments, as in early biblical times, were standing, talking quietly at the far end of the room, which opened toward the right, in an L-shape.

A huge man with a short beard and balding pate, his brown robe cinched with a rope, strode directly to me and held out an empty mug. When he turned to walk away, I set the mug on the table and took a deep breath. I was pleased; evidently I was a young serving girl or boy who would be unnoticed. I could explore. I began to walk toward the far end of the room then I realized that the people were waiting to learn if Jesus was dead. I thought, *It must be Good Friday or Easter Sunday. If Mary is here the news will devastate her. All these people will be in great distress. I know that Jesus died on the cross.*

I saw Mary P, who was a friend from high school. She stood with the others, talking. She wore a long, blue and white garment. We made eye contact, with a strange zoom-like effect I had experienced before. She did not say anything, nor did I, thinking she was also there as an observer. I felt a stab of pain for Jesus' mother when I heard, "Yes, he is dead," then I felt a tug, and returned to my bed at home.

This past-life experience raised a number of questions. Why had I felt such a need to be inconspicuous? Why did I go to that particular time and place? What was I to learn? One lesson may be that what seems like the end, can also be a beginning. Jesus died, but his resurrection changed the spiritual beliefs of many. I resolved to find the answer to my first question at a later time. I was, and still am, amazed and thrilled that Jesus prayed with me.

I was also curious about Mary P's presence in that room. My recollection of her in school is of a friendly, quiet girl who made good grades, was active in religious activities and worked on the school paper. Most of my contact with her was during the year she played with me on the basketball team. I hadn't known her well, but our fathers became friends through the Fathers Club. Maybe that was our connection. She has also been in several of my dreams, which added to my puzzlement. Several years later we discussed them at a school reunion, which I'll write about in chapter twenty-three.

A few weeks later I left my body and came to a small wooden house surrounded by water. It felt like a past life, but I did not know where, or even who I was. Other houses nearby were flooded and empty. I called for help, but there was no answer. I wondered if everyone was dead. I was wearing a long, black skirt, covered with a white cotton apron. A catastrophe had occurred and I had survived; learning nothing more, I returned to my body.

On another night I had gone to bed early, and by 6 a.m. I was wide awake. I decided to meditate, and wondered what would be different if I went OOB in daylight. I shifted my position and tried to quiet my mind then felt vibrations, heard the familiar buzzing, and saw flashes of light. I felt something expand inside, with an electrical, tingling sensation. I lifted out, flew into the sky, and heard voices say, "OK. Good." I asked for guidance or help. My hands were translucent. I was out in space, alert and full of anticipation. Dropping toward land, I saw a building and went inside. The floor underneath my bare feet was cool marble. People were preparing food and eating. They couldn't see me. I flew out a window and over lush, green grass, bordered by rolling hills. A young gardener, dressed in black and white, wearing a black hat, stood in the center of the lawn. He seemed familiar, and was aware of my presence. Birds began to sing, and I wondered if they were back in Dallas. I was in both places at once then I was home.

Several years later, in Florence, Italy, I spent an afternoon with a friend at the Pitti Palace and the Boboli gardens. I had a strong sense of déjà vu, recognizing the lawn as the one in the previous experience with the young man clipping grass for the Medici family, whose gardens these were, centuries earlier.

Another experience gave me some understanding of my place in the universe. I'd asked my spirit guides to help me learn, then focused on my breathing. After a short time, I let go, sat up and stepped out of body. The light in the bedroom was dim as I moved toward my dresser and peered into the mirror. My image faded and changed to another face, then to another and another —a dozen faces. I felt that all the men and women I saw in the mirror were people I had been in past lives. Some were stern, plain and serious; others were young, softer. Catching something in my peripheral vision, I turned, and was startled to see a tall, thin man standing next to me. He was dressed like a court jester, a trickster, and was lighting and flicking matches into the air. Feeling threatened, I called for help to get him to leave. He disappeared and I returned to my body.

A couple of years later, at a workshop on past life recall I learned more the above experience. Dr. Brian Weiss, author of Many Lives, Many Masters, described mirror gazing, in which a series of faces from past lives evolves. In addition, he said we can also see others' past lives. Each of us paired with someone we did not know, and sat, relaxed, facing our partner in the large, dimly lit room, gazing at each other in silence. Most of us experienced the phenomena of seeing faces appear, dissolve and change.

I was stunned at the variety of images I saw in my partner, from a small brown boy, young women and old men, to a beautiful light-haired woman, draped in blue, with a large white halo around her. She looked like paintings of Mary, Jesus' mother. Her face was visible for several seconds.

That afternoon Dr. Weiss suggested a group exercise in which we seek a past life recall to answer questions we might have. The question I hoped to answer was why I felt the need to keep my spiritual beliefs secret in this life and others, including my life around the time of Jesus' death. To my surprise I relaxed quickly, then flew into a past-life experience; I had been captured for being a disciple of Christ and was in a large arena or coliseum. A lion was released to attack me, but instead it walked over and held up its paw. I removed something from it; the lion was quite docile. (I realize this sounds like a cliché, but I guess that's because such things did happen).

A man seated in a place of power became angry at having been deprived of the spectacle of seeing me torn apart, and sent gladiators into the ring to kill me. As they got close, weapons raised, I was pulled up and away from my body, and knew that I had nothing to fear. This experience helped explain my pattern of apprehension, both past and present, in exposing my spiritual beliefs and the paranormal events in my life. I need to remind myself that even in that coliseum I was protected and was not alone.

***

I learned something else about past lives in a dream: *I was a young, southern woman walking home in the cold of winter. I heard a noise under the porch of a small house, and shined light onto a quilt; it was moving. A whole family of slaves hid under it. I took them home with me and hid them until they could escape to the north.*

Soon after that dream, a psychic told me I had spent another life helping slaves escape through the Underground Railroad. He said I'd spent many lifetimes acting as a conduit, or bridge, for those moving from one place to another, physically or emotionally. As usual, I was skeptical, but what he said did have a familiar feel.

TEN

The angels keep their ancient places.
Turn but a stone, and start a wing.
Francis Thompson

Wonderful mysteries present themselves to us throughout our lives if we are open to them. The earliest I recall, a small one, happened on a bright, summer morning when I was ten or eleven years old, a pig-tailed, freckled, skinny tomboy. Wearing striped t-shirt and blue jeans, I was riding my bike the two miles to visit my grandparents at their small farm. I noticed something glittering in the center of the blacktop road and coasted toward it. Three coins were stacked there—a half-dollar, a quarter and a nickel. The money was sitting too neatly to have fallen by accident. If dropped carelessly, the coins would have rolled toward the edge of the road. I decided they were a gift, picked them up, put them in my pocket and rode on. Finding that money reinforced my belief that the world is a friendly place and reminded me to notice things around me and expect surprises.

These gentle reminders to pay attention often trigger questions about the nature of the universe. Many events in our lives cannot be explained by the law of cause and effect. Some-times we overlook mystery/miracles or we find reasons to dis-count them. We don't want to be considered superstitious. In the manual used by mental health professionals to categorize emotional, thinking, and behavioral disorders, symptoms of schizophrenia include referential delusions—the belief that comments, passages from books or newspapers or other environ-mental cues are directed specifically at one. Yet haven't we all had a question in mind, then picked up a book or magazine, or turned on television or the radio and read or heard an answer to that very question?

The sabbatical I mentioned earlier centered around a twelve day writers' conference at Vermont's Burlington College mountaintop campus. Afterward, I spent six weeks at my brother's house in the mountains of south Vermont. I had few neighbors, none within walking distance. I could read and write undisturbed while soaking in the beauty of the changing autumn leaves. I'd been a little apprehensive about staying there alone, having always been surrounded by loving family and friends. It helped that John and his family usually drove up from Boston on weekends, staying one night.

It did not take long to adjust. Reading, writing, taking long walks every day and watching green leaves change to scarlet and gold as Vermont's 'leaf-peeping' season began filled my days. I watched for the deer that I knew populated the woods. In the mornings there would be hoof prints in the yard, but no deer made an appearance. I had read that they were shy, and more likely to be spotted at dusk or dawn, so several mornings I got up before dawn and sat in the dark, sipping hot lemon-mint tea as I watched out the kitchen window. Still no deer.

One Saturday my brother and I set off in his old blue truck, over narrow mountain roads for the nearest town, to pick up groceries. When I told John I was disappointed not to have seen any deer, he said we could get up at four a.m. the next day and walk to a glade that attracted deer. The idea held little appeal to me. In true big sister fashion, I said, "But I want to see a deer *now!*" just as we drove around a curve.

A huge, full-antlered buck was standing in the middle of the road. John slammed on the brakes, his eyes wide. We sat and stared at the deer, which stood gazing at us for about a minute then walked regally to the side of the road toward a doe and two fawns. Upon reaching them he paused, we stared at each other for fifteen or twenty seconds more, then they all turned and vanished into the woods.

As my friend, Marguerite, says, "It never hurts to ask for

what you want, to express it clearly, then put it out to the universe and release it." Often we receive a response instantly, which reminds us to pay closer attention and listen for an answer, even to expect one.

***

My daughter and I found numerous synchronicities when we spent a month in Europe. For instance, we walked onto the grounds of Edinburgh Castle just as the bag-pipers started playing and marching. Then they shot off cannons in a twenty-one-gun salute. We joked that it was for us, but found out later that it was Prince Charles' birthday. And we arrived in Lucerne, Switzerland, on the only night of their big summer festival.

A week earlier, when the conductor on a train to York very diplomatically told us we were in a first class car but had second class tickets, another passenger, a woman from York intervened. She said, "It's all right. They're Americans." He nodded and walked on. Then the woman told us about the Mystery Plays, held every four years. It was the last night, and was sold out, but she was sure we could get tickets by going to the side gate exactly twenty minutes before the start of the play.

"They always hold back eight tickets for "very special people, such as yourselves," she said.

She also told us it would rain that night, but would stop in time for the Plays. We were not sure what qualified us as "very special people." Maybe it was just that we were Americans, but she was right about the tickets. And the rain that started a couple of hours earlier did indeed stop five minutes before the play started. Our whole month in Europe and on the British Isles had gone that way.

A few years later, my friend, Susie, experienced similar synchronicities on a trip to Europe. Our trip was the result of some interesting coincidences. Susie's son had won two tickets to fly to Zurich, but was unable to use them, so he gave them to his parents. Susie's husband didn't want to go, and she asked me if I would like to join her. I didn't hesitate. We stayed in Switzerland for a few days then took a train to Florence, Italy, an artist's treasure trove. Susie is an artist. What could be more perfect? We found many moments of serendipity, exhausted ourselves walking the cobblestone streets, got lost, but never for long, and made new friends. We visited Kusnaught, the small town outside Zurich where Carl Jung had lived and we toured the Jungian Institute, with its bountiful gardens, as well as the cemetery.

The synchronicities continued after our return home. We were walking near her house through a wooded area, trying to work off the chocolate we'd eaten in Zurich. After almost an hour, we came to a new street, with houses under construction. Interested in a nearly completed house, we wandered through it, opening closets and cabinet doors, commenting on what we liked and didn't like. As we left and walked toward the street, Susie asked if Dean and I were thinking of moving to a new house. I said no, but that I'd love to buy some land in the Colorado mountains and build a house there.

She said, "Texas has some really pretty areas too, with hills and trees."

"Not hills. Mountains! I need mountains," I said.

"Then we'll just have to get you mountains," she said.

We stepped out of the yard into the street, and almost on top of a large painting lying at the edge of the yard. It was a nicely framed picture of mountains, trees and water. We stood, staring at it, unmoving, neither of us speaking for a minute. Susie said, "There are your mountains."

The painting was dusty, but not damaged. It had probably fallen off a pick-up truck days earlier. Although the mountains in the picture weren't quite what I had visualized, Susie convinced me I could paint over them and make them "my" mountains, which is what she helped me do. Instead of the gray, lone mountain peak and gray sky, I now have purple mountains tipped with snow, a blue sky with pink and white clouds, and more trees.

ELEVEN

*Success is a journey, not a destination. The doing
is often more important than the outcome.*
Arthur Ashe

Mom stayed in Belleville for a year and a half after Dad died.
When we moved her to Dallas, I was torn between the wish to
bring her to our house to live and the reality that she needed
more care than Dean and I could give her. She told us that she
wanted to live *near* us, not *with* us. We tried to make the assisted
living apartment cheerful and home-like, but Mom never did
adjust to taking the elevator to the dining room. She was afraid
to ride on it alone and was confused with the up/down buttons.

A series of small strokes wiped out her ability to manipulate
anything mechanical or technical. Mom would lock her door and
be unable to open it, then panic and knock, calling for help until
someone heard her, located a key, opened the door and calmed
her down. She forgot how to use the phone and could not relearn
the skill. She could still hold a conversation, but anything she
had to manipulate was beyond her grasp. She worried a lot about
making mistakes or not knowing how to do something, so I
spent much of our time together reassuring her that she need not
be concerned about them. It was easier for me to say than for her
to stop worrying.

Over the next few years, as a result of the strokes and
Alzheimer's disease, Mom lost her ability to walk, the use of one
hand, and finally the other. As her needs grew, we moved her to
a nursing home only five minutes from our house. We visited
often, sometimes more than once a day. It was a painful time for

everyone who loved her, and depressing to be able to do so little for her.

We struggled with the nursing home staff, trying to get them to understand and fulfill her needs, especially since Mom could not push the call-light button. I told them, wrote notes, asked nicely and not-so-nicely to please check on her, give her water to drink, brush her teeth, take her to the bathroom, wash her hands, and take her to the musical programs she loved that were held in the dining room.

The nurses and aides said she was the sweetest person there, but that didn't always translate into getting help when she needed it. Mom was not used to complaining. I wasn't either, but I learned. Sometime the squeaky door *does* get the oil. I felt emotionally and physically drained, but I found spiritual comfort in our intense, close contact. Sometimes I felt I could see and know everything she was thinking and needed. She gave her unconditional love as freely as ever. I still feel the power of it.

Mom's short-term memory gradually deteriorated until it was almost non-existent. Until the end, she retained her smile, her thoughtfulness and the desire to help others. When anyone came into the room, she would greet them and look around for something to offer, such as cookies or tea. She tried to help the aides, and thanked them for everything they did. I learned a lot about courage, love and strength from her during that time.

Mom was depressed. I was beginning to be depressed too. One afternoon, before visiting Mom, I attended a group discussion with a friend. The topic was the connection between science and the spiritual. The guest speaker, a psychic, told me my concern and empathy for others led me to 'taking on' other people's depression, and it was becoming a problem for me. He was right. Besides my sadness about Mom, I'd had difficulty lately leaving my clients' problems at the office. The young man added that I would soon hear something that would help me and that I should listen.

"Really listen." I nodded, and he repeated it. "Listen."

I nodded again. "Yes. I will."

After the meeting, I got in my car to drive to the nursing

home and turned on the radio. The first thing I heard was a man's voice say, "Now listen to this!"

That got my attention! A beautiful song I'd never heard before filled the car. It began, "If I could, I'd protect you from the sadness in your eyes," and related, in a powerful way, that we can't remove someone else's pain by taking it on ourselves. That message was exactly what I needed. I glanced at the radio dial and made a mental note to tune in to that station again. I felt much better, lighter, less burdened. I thought the song had been a wonderful gift to me from spirit or my angel. "Thank you!" I said out loud.

Later that night, on reflection, I thought the song had *probably* been a gift. The next day, when I got in the car to visit Mom again, I remembered how sad I had been the day before and how the word 'listen' from the young man at the meeting, then again in the car, had focused my attention fully on the song that had calmed my troubled emotions. It may or may not have been played especially for me at that time, but it had been a helpful coincidence. Then I turned the radio on, and my 'Doubting Thomas' belief system got a jolt when the beginning notes of 'If I Could' filled the car again.

"OK," I said. "I get it." I'm sure I smiled. On my way home that day I stopped at a store and bought the CD, so I could share the song with others. A few days later, when I turned the car radio on, a brand new country-western station occupied that spot on the dial. The other station was gone, right after I received a message I needed to hear. Twice.

A year later, as her condition worsened, it was hard for Mom to respond to the simplest questions or even to speak at all. I had been struggling with the loss of her ability to communicate verbally. She seemed to be disappearing, bit by bit. I was already grieving. I prayed for help.

Not long after, a friend brought to my attention an A.R.E. (Association for Research and Enlightenment) research project on synchronicity. I was curious, but had no particular expectations. I was in for a few surprises.

The study was simple. I was to listen to a short tape, then

write down each day any coincidences I noticed. That's all, just take notice and write them down. The second week I listened to another short tape then continued recording. The third tape said to continue to note coincidences, to visualize asking a question of a wise man or woman, and that week I would discover the answer to my question.

As might be expected, just paying attention increased the number of coincidences I noticed, but the sheer number of them amazed me. One morning in particular, every time I thought of someone, the phone would ring and it would be that person. This happened over and over. At one point, I dug out a list of former clients, thinking I would call or write some of them as a follow-up to their therapy. I picked up a pen and put a check mark next to one of the names, a young woman, Anne, whom I had not talked with in several months. The phone rang. It was Anne, calling me for the first and only time at my home. I noticed an increase in synchronicity as I paid more attention to it. As I validated experiences, they became part of my belief system. When I finished the study, I filled out the requested report, describing the many events during those weeks that did not fit ordinary coincidence. I left the completed study on my desk for over a week. When I noticed it, I thought there must be some reason I hadn't mailed it. It could wait a few more days. Some coincidences are neither mystery nor miracle, but ...

One morning, while taking a long walk, I was thinking about Mom's decline, pondering whether there was anything more we, her family, could do to help her. I finally admitted to myself that our relationship would never again be as it had been. I had always treasured her wisdom and the example she set, but now she had to struggle to express even her most basic needs. Although I had not, in word or actions, expressed my hope that she might even briefly, be herself again, we were so tuned in to each other emotionally and spiritually I knew she could feel how much I missed her old self. I let go.

Later that day, driving to work, I noticed an ad on a large billboard. It said "Success Is the Journey, Not the Destination." Ten minutes later I was walking down the hall toward my office when I nearly ran into the open door of a cleaning supply closet. Facing me was a trash-can with a bumper sticker across the front that read: *Success is the Journey, Not the Destination.* I noted the coincidence. Later, a client was talking about changes he wanted to make in his life. I said I was reminded of a saying.

He interrupted. "Yes. Something like success is not the destination, but the journey."

"You saw that bumper sticker on the trash can too!"

"No." He didn't know what I was talking about. He had not seen the bumper sticker. He said he had just been thinking about the importance of being able to appreciate the struggles in life's journey, and not wish them away. *More coincidence.*

Musing about coincidences and synchronicity as I drove home, I soon shifted my thoughts to dinner, and the paperwork I wanted to finish that evening. When I walked into the kitchen, I dropped my briefcase and purse on the table then noticed several pieces of note-book paper on the edge of the kitchen counter. Even without reading glasses I recognized Mother's Palmer-method handwriting. I wondered where those scraps of paper had come from and what they were doing on the counter. I asked my husband. He'd never seen them before. We never did find out how those papers got there.

I dug my glasses out of my purse, and saw four journal entries, written by Mom twelve years earlier, each a month apart. I'd seen no signs of a journal before, nor have I seen any since that night. The first page was dated December 5, 1980. It riveted my attention.

It began: *Thoughts while sitting waiting in the dentist's chair…There is a plaque on the wall that reads, "Dental Health, like Success, is not a destination but a Continuous Journey." I like to be observant of my surroundings. . .*

I was shocked and thrilled. Each entry was special to me. The second, dated January 1, 1981 held a bit of a picture of her own growing-up years. She wrote:

I wake up this morning thinking of New Year's Day at home. Happy New Year was the good word of the morning. Everyone wanted to be first saying it. We had a small house but it was full of everyone talking—noise. I now wonder at the patience of my parents. Mother was always interested in all of the chatter. You had to talk loud and fast to be heard. One thing, life was never dull.

Reading this gave me a warm feeling about what a long, loving life Mom had. The third page began like a journal entry, but at the end it seemed like a letter, as if Mom knew I would be reading it someday.

Today we received a beautiful book that Marilyn wrote. Such pride and joy Dad and I felt, reminiscing about our daughter's birth, growth and development. I remember the day she was born. It was hot as blazes. Dr. Hurd and his wife were at the Majestic theatre and you were in a hurry to be born. The nurse told me to hold my breath! Wait for the Dr!? When he arrived, he rolled up his sleeves and said everything is all right. That's all I remember till I saw you. You were beautiful.

The book Mom received that day was one I had written with a friend and mentor, Dr. Dan Perkins. The last journal entry I found on my kitchen counter was written on March 10, 1981, Mom's birthday. She wrote,

I'm 73 years old—am wondering where the time went. My wish is for health and the courage to grow old gracefully— happiness for all our dear family. Our children are our pride and joy and their children are precious.

I knew when I read those journal entries I would always benefit from my mother's wisdom if I paid attention.

TWELVE

Be realistic. Plan for a miracle.
Bagwan Shree Rajneesh

At an intuition workshop I attended I expected to learn how to improve knowledge of my inner self, but there was an unexpected bonus. The presenters showed us how to access helpful information for others, which I felt would aid me when counseling clients.

Over two hundred people filled the lecture room, and we were asked to partner with someone we didn't know. I felt drawn to a woman several rows away. She was also gravitating toward me. We didn't talk with each other, except to say hello, then we were asked to close our eyes, breathe, relax and clear our minds of all thought, so that only information for our partner would come in. She said not to worry that we wouldn't 'get' anything, that nobody's mind can stay blank for long. We might see pictures, hear words, or have random thoughts come into our minds, and were not to interpret what we got, just blurt it out, whatever it was.

My partner and I sat facing one another, eyes closed. We were to give no feedback during the reading. When we finished we shared our reactions to what was said. My partner told me I had hit on images that reflected important concerns in her life, especially about her granddaughter and her own meditation practice. What she reported to me fit as well.

We 'read' from photos we'd brought of someone we knew well. I'd brought one of my daughter, Susan. We did not discuss the people in the photos, but wrote what we 'intuited' about our partner's photo. We were to visualize going back into a past life of the person—their life, attitudes, experience, beliefs, etc. Then we were to 'go through a door' to a second past life, then a third. We wrote briefly about each experience before we shared what we had seen with our partners. What I wrote about my partner's granddaughter seemed accurate to her.

I was surprised when I saw what she had written about Susan. She had not seen her past lives, but parts of her present life. First she saw a happy, loving little girl about seven years old, with long blond hair, in a sort of 'Heidi' dress, with a white ruffled apron, white socks and black Mary Jane shoes. The second image was a young woman in her early twenties, in college, working as a waitress, who was happy, loving and funny, and who "never gave a thought to the meaning of the word responsibility." These were all true of Susan, including the last vision she had of a woman in middle life.

Later, another woman asked me for impressions of her husband. She had brought a picture of him. I focused on the picture then closed my eyes. I saw what looked like three points of a star; the bottom of it obscured by a line or wall, and a side-walk, trees and vague rooflines of houses. As I was about to open my eyes, I felt an intense sensation of heaviness in my chest. When I told her what I'd seen, she said her husband builds houses. Then I showed her the sketch I'd made of the 'star.' She dug her husband's business card out of her purse. In the upper left corner was a crown that looked like a star, with three-points showing; the bottom of the star was hidden by a house. I told her of the heaviness I'd felt in my chest, she said her husband had been worried and depressed lately, that he had a 'heavy heart.' Both workshops were aimed at connecting to our own intuition and to Universal Spirit.

***

Paying closer attention to my inner voice has been of great benefit to me, and late one Friday evening, I had reason to be especially grateful for help I received from spirit. My clients rarely call me on weekends, but they sometimes leave messages on my answering machine, usually about changing an appointment or asking me to remind them of something at their next counseling session. They have a different number to call in case of emergency.

That night, at about 11:30, I put down the book I was reading and started toward the hall and our bedroom. Dean had already turned in and the house was quiet. I picked up the phone to check for messages one last time and was surprised to hear Patti L's voice. I had seen her a few times with her husband, Stan, who suffered from a chronic pain condition and struggled with anger, depression and guilt.

His doctors worked constantly to try and balance his medical and psychological needs and had made progress, but he had been traveling lately for his job. I hadn't seen him in several weeks.

The message from Patti was simple: call her when I had a chance. She sounded calm. It was a couple of hours since she had called, and ordinarily I would have waited until morning to phone her, but something told me not to wait. I dialed the number and after several rings, Stan answered.

"Hello?" His voice sounded slurred and I wondered if he had been drinking.

"Hello, Stan. This is Marilyn. Is Patti there? I'm returning her call."

"No, she's gone." He paused then said, "They're here now. In the yard. I guess you called them."

"Who's in the yard? Called who, Stan?" I asked.

"The police. Isn't that why you called me?"

"I called you because I just now heard a message Patti left me a couple of hours ago. What are the police doing there?"

"Oh. Then I guess one of the neighbors called."

"Why are the police there, Stan?" I asked again. I could feel my heartbeat accelerating. "And where are Patti and the boys?"

"I did a terrible thing." He started to cry. I had to strain to hear his words over the sobs. "I got mad at Patti then I started drinking. I accused her of liking some other guy. I know that's crazy. But I was jealous. She got mad at me for what I said and we got in a fight. I took out some guns and started shooting up the house and the garage. They're gone now. It's all my fault."

67

His voice was slurring again and his sobbing grew louder.

"Patti and the boys! Where are they?" I asked.

"My God. Bullet holes everywhere. I must be nuts."

"Stan!" I said. "Patti. The boys. Where are they?"

"Probably at her Mom and Dad's. They left after I shot up the house. Her folks will take care of them. They're better off without me anyway. I can't do anything right." His sobs grew louder. "I've really done it this time, Marilyn. I can't fix it now. It's over."

He paused and I jumped in, relieved to hear that Patti and their two young sons all right. But Stan sounded suicidal.

"Stan, why do you think I called you now, just when the police pulled up?"

There was a pause. "That is weird," he said. "I just walked inside from shooting up the garage. I wouldn't have heard the phone from out there. And in another minute I would have been going out the front door with a gun in my hand. Wouldn't hear any more phones then."

He'd been in despair and had given up. He had planned to walk out the door carrying a gun, provoking the police to shoot him. Suicide, without having to pull the trigger.

He was crying again. "It's too late. I really screwed up this time. Patti must hate me now. It's over."

"It is not over, Stan. I'm telling you it is not over. I called you, didn't I?"

"Yeah. And you didn't know what was going on here?" He sounded puzzled, momentarily deflected from his plan to end everything.

There was no time to think about what to say, to change the script he'd written in his mind. He could not live up to the ideals he'd set for himself. I knew he was deeply religious and I suspected that he felt God could not forgive him. I didn't think. The words just came. "I know you believe in God," I said.

"Yes, but I …"

"I know you believe in God, and He doesn't want you to die now. There's no way I could have known exactly when to call you, unless God wanted me to tell you not to do this, not to let yourself be killed."

"You think God doesn't want me to do this? Maybe you are right. You called, and you're probably the only person I would have listened to."

"Yes."

"I'm so tired," he said. "I don't know what to do. I guess they do though," referring to the policemen in his front yard.

"Yes they do. Stan, will you listen to me and do exactly what I tell you?"

"Yes."

"Do you have a gun in your hand?"

"No. I put it down when I answered the phone. But there are fifteen or twenty of them lying all over the room."

"Do not pick up a gun. And don't hang up the phone. Is the porch light on?"

"Yes."

"Leave it on. In a minute I want you to go outside. But first, listen. Keep your empty hands in front of you where the police can see them. Leave all the lights on. Open the door and walk out, holding your hands up and in front of you. They don't want to shoot you."

"I know. They'll probably take me to jail. That's OK. Maybe I can get some rest," he said. "I'm ready."

"Yes, you are. If you have the chance, tell the policeman you're on the phone with your counselor and that if he would talk to me for a minute, I would appreciate it." I paused. "Now, take a deep breath, put the phone down, open the front door, and let the police take over."

"I will. Thank you, Marilyn." Stan was polite to me, as always. There was a click when he set the phone on the table.

After a long silence, I heard, "This is Officer Lorenz."

It was over. During the call I'd felt calm once I knew Patti and the boys were safe, and afterwards I was still calm, knowing my inner spirit had directed my words. After I hung up the phone, I went to bed and fell asleep immediately. The police took Stan to the hospital emergency room. When he was allowed to have visitors a couple of days later, I went to see him. He thanked me again, and said that if I had not called at exactly that time, he knew he would be dead. He and his wife both believe that my call was the result of God's intervention. I thank God that I've learned to listen to intuition, my inner self, and the angels.

I was beginning to understand how Dorothy must have felt when she found herself in Oz. Growing up in the secure midst of a loving family in the Midwest, I had taken many things for granted, including my faith. Then I was blown off course by the winds of change, and on my journey I found the unusual, the beautiful, the mundane, and the strange; at times I was disappointed, at times delighted, but found my path by recognizing, like Dorothy did with a click of her red shoes, that what I was looking for was always there. I had only to open my eyes to see. When I began having experiences that diminished my skepticism, they gave wings to my spiritual understanding and fostered a rediscovery of beliefs I had long doubted or had forgotten.

THIRTEEN

Every spirit builds itself a house, and beyond its house,
a world, and beyond its world, a heaven. Know then,
that world exists for you. Ralph Waldo Emerson

Before I attended a dowser conference with Marguerite I
knew almost nothing about dowsers. I learned they not only
locate water and other things by connecting with spirit, but they
read auras, receive answers to questions asked, and use their
skills for healing.

The first speaker said we all have the ability to see auras, and
she would teach us how to see these halos of light. She followed
through on her promise. Since that night I often see light around
others. The same speaker showed us how to bend spoons and we
took turns bending rebars (reinforcing bars) with a partner. We
would each hold an end of the rebar, gaze at the center and walk
toward each other, visualizing the steel bar bending. I still have
my bent rebar. One woman was upset because she and her
partner couldn't do it. I noticed that her glasses were broken and
she didn't look directly at the center of the rebar. She didn't have
confidence that it would work, so it didn't. I offered to do it with
her, and told her why I thought it hadn't worked the first time.

"It doesn't matter if you can't see it well. Just tell yourself
you can do it, gaze at the center of the bar and walk toward me.
It will work." I don't know why I was so confident, but sometimes … I just know—and it did work. We can do many things if
we believe.

Besides bending rebars and spoons, and 'seeing' another's
aura, we can work with the aura to facilitate healing. I attended a

workshop designed to demonstrate such healing.

When I signed up for it, it was with mild curiosity, but by the time it began, my interest was more than cursory. Whether from the smoky corridors, exhaustion, or something else, I wasn't feeling good that day. The right side of my head, my right eye, my sinuses—in fact, the entire right side of my body hurt. The longer I sat in the crowded room, the worse I felt.

The presenter, Ed, was to demonstrate a healing on a volunteer, but first he discussed various facets of dowsing, then answered questions. It looked as if there would be no time for him to demonstrate. Finally he glanced at his watch, said we had better start and asked for a volunteer. I was seated near the back of the room, and half the people raised their hands. By then I felt terrible. I didn't know what he was going to do, but if he could do something to diminish my pain, I wanted his help. I focused on getting his attention, caught his eye and waved my hand, thinking he *has* to choose me. He did. My head hurt so much I wasn't even embarrassed to stand in front of the room as a guinea pig.

Ed explained energy healing worked by balancing the aura. First he measured my aura from the front, back and both sides, using a copper dowsing rod. When he walked toward me from each direction, the rod would hold steady until it came in contact with my aura, then it would swing back as my aura blocked the dowsing rod. One side was much closer than the other.

Without touching me, using gestures you might use to fluff then smooth something, he balanced my aura. As he did, he explained what he was doing to the other workshop attendees. I felt a sort of crinkling sensation in the right side of my head as the pain began to dissolve. My whole body felt better. Then it felt as if the right side of my head was growing outward. I wondered briefly if anyone could *see* my head grow, but rationalized that the feeling of expansion must be my aura, becoming more balanced.

A few minutes later, Ed stopped, said it was time for the next workshop and thanked everyone for coming. As they left the room, he asked me how I felt and suggested I sit for a minute or two, saying that I looked a little dizzy. I thanked him, reached for his hand to shake, and was startled to feel intense vibration, though our clasped hands did not appear to move. A minute later, as I sat on a folding chair near the front of the room, I watched Ed gather his papers, preparing to leave. I told him about the crinkling sensation, the feeling that my head was growing and my pain was gone. His reply was caring, but casual, saying I would probably notice some healing off and on over the next couple of weeks. It was evident he was not surprised.

I had a question. "Did you feel vibration when I took your hand?"

"Yes."

Recently I had been experiencing a sensation of higher or more rapid vibration when I was in bed and in an altered state of consciousness, but I didn't know what to make of it. Nothing I'd read explained it and I hadn't met anyone else who mentioned vibration. It was not the sort of thing I had known how to ask about, or who to ask.

"Does it have something to do with healing?"

"Yes, it does. When you channel healing energy, you often feel vibration. Sometimes you feel intense heat." Ed gathered his books and briefcase and glanced at the door, ready to move on.

"Thanks again," I said. "I'm fine. I'm just going to stay here a few more minutes."

After he left, I sat alone, soaking up a feeling of calmness and well-being. I watched and listened, during the next workshop on experiential healing, but did not participate much. When I told the presenter I was still healing from the previous session she smiled and said she could see that. It was the young woman who had demonstrated the ability to see auras on the first night. This time she emphasized the importance of the healer getting his or her own ego out of the way and having the intent of healing for the highest good.

She explained that we have several layers of auras. The dense, etheric field is closest to the body. Next is the astral field, which holds our prana. The thinnest of the three fields is the mental or emotional body, which does not conform to our body shape, but completely surrounds us, as if we are suspended inside a large, oval 'egg' of light. Resolving problems in our energy fields prevent those problems from developing in the physical body.

After the conference I could see that by connecting with my clients' auras through my heart chakra, they more easily reached emotional and spiritual well-being. In her book Second Sight, psychiatrist Judith Orloff wrote that she realized if she did not use all her talents and skills, including intuition, she would not be honoring her vow to not only do no harm, but also to seek a therapeutic relationship in which she could give her all. I was also fortunate to hear her speak. Despite sitting toward the back of a room filled with hundreds of people, I could feel the strength of her positive energy as she spoke. She was surrounded by incredible light—her aura. I'm sure she has inspired many to more fully use their own gifts.

Including spiritual issues as part of psychotherapy has become more common, as therapists and clients recognize that existential struggles about inner life are crucial to personal growth. Being listened to without criticism or demands helps fill a deep yearning everyone has to understand ourselves and to be understood. Focusing on the heart chakra adds to the positive energy in therapy, and inner truths are more easily accessed at this spiritual level. There is tremendous light around some healers, whether emotional, spiritual or physical, as they connect with their inner self and their spirit helpers.

* * *

Learning to see auras led me to a wonderful experience in Angel Fire, New Mexico, where I attended a writers' conference. I stayed at a friend's house while there. On Sunday she and her husband attended mass at San Francisco de Asis, an old Catholic church in Ranchos de Taos. I went with them, eager to see the church that was the subject of many wonderful Georgia O'Keefe paintings.

It was the week of *enjare*, when parishioners patch and repair the adobe church. Ladders leaned against the building and supplies were piled everywhere. The inside of the church was also being painted and repaired. We entered through a side door, and skirted around the furniture stacked in the small hallway that led to the body of the church. The thick, old hymnal I picked up had a solid feel to it. Stepping onto brown paper laid to protect the wood floors, we crunched our way to the second pew, where we had an unimpeded view of the altar. Behind the altar, paintings of Jesus, Mary and the saints gleamed brilliantly in vivid blues, golds, and reds, and the scent of flowers wafting toward me was heavenly. I knelt for a few minutes, then sat, and was instantly filled with peace and a heightened sense of awareness.

When services began, we joined the congregation in singing old, familiar hymns. There was no accompaniment that day; none was needed as the church filled with song. A woman directly behind me had a beautiful voice that evoked memories of my childhood, and sitting next to my mother, with her sweet soprano voice. When a nun walked to the lectern to read the homily, a bright halo of light encircled her head. I glanced toward the priest, the deacon and the server girls, sitting at the side altar. They all had light around their heads; the smallest girl seemed to be encased in a huge oval of light. Bright balls of light also glowed on the altar, like angels dancing. (When I mentioned the lights to my friend later, she was surprised. She hadn't seen the lights, nor had her husband.)

Mass ended and I left reluctantly, walking out slowly as we sang the recessional hymn, *Ode to Joy*. I'd found myself, full circle, home again. I was not ready to leave. Catching up with my friends, I said I wanted to go through the front door to see the whole church. I edged through the crowd that was leaving then knelt in a back pew, soaking in the feel of the morning. When I went back outside, I stood in line to exchange greetings with the priest and the deacon, wanting to tell them what a special morning it had been, but there was no need for words. They knew this was a blessed place, filled with love and light.

Memories of that peaceful, joyous morning fill my heart, residing there to lift my spirit when I stumble or when the road seems steep.

FOURTEEN

Life is either a daring adventure or nothing.
Helen Keller

At the dowser's conference, every workshop and lecture I attended offered a new experience. By lunchtime on the last day, my mind was spinning with ideas. I needed time to slow down and think about nothing more challenging than making a choice between soup and salad. I had thought about skipping the afternoon workshops, but decided to stay. I did not want to miss anything. The program said something about communication with spirits. Fifty or sixty people filled the brightly lit room.

The speaker, Laura, explained psychometry, a process in which, by holding another's possession, like a watch or ring, one can intuit or sense something about him or her. We each teamed up with someone we didn't know, then held our partner's ring or watch or other item, and closed our eyes. I envisioned a girl's face, and something shaped like a banana or new moon. I also saw a tree leaning against a wooden fence that seemed to be a problem for her. My partner was amazed. She said her favorite picture of her daughter was in a picture frame shaped like the new moon. She also said she had been worried and angry because her neighbor's tree was about to knock her fence down and they would not do anything about it. When we switched roles, she described several things she saw, one of which was pencils. She asked if I was a writer, which I am. The other items she visualized also made sense to me.

After the psychometry exercise, Laura talked about spirits, saying they are always around us, that there were many in the room, and they wanted to contact us. After leading us through a brief relaxation exercise, she told us to picture a person in the spirit world we'd like to hear from. I visualized my dad. *He will surely want to talk to me if he is around,* I thought. *If spirits can communicate with us, my dad will be the first one to get a message through.* He was never shy.

Laura told us to erase the picture we had envisioned and open our eyes. She asked all spirits to communicate only for the highest good then said there was a spirit in the room who was especially eager to speak. "Who has a Jim or James on the other side?"

I was the only one to raise my hand. My dad, James, was also called Jim. Laura said he was pointing to his chest, and she asked if he'd had something wrong there.

I nodded. "He died of congestive heart failure."

"Was his death unexpected?"

"Sort of. He lived 'til ninety, so it shouldn't have been unexpected, but it was. He'd been in the hospital for one day, and when I called from Dallas that night, the nurse said he was doing better. The next morning Dad was gone."

Laura said he was fine now, that he was laughing and saying, "Don't worry about me. Worry about you. Don't work so much. Enjoy yourself. Have some fun." She said there was something she couldn't quite understand, but it sounded like, "Have fun playing...basketball?"

"Yes!" One of the joys of my life was playing basketball in high school, and Dad had been my biggest booster, bragging about it to strangers at supermarkets and drugstores years later. He sent a message he knew I would understand. When Laura asked if I had questions for Dad, I could not think of any. I said no, thanked her, and sat back, satisfied.

Then she said that a Margaret, or Maggie, was there. It was my grandmother (Dad's mother). Once again, I was the only one to raise my hand. Laura said Margaret and Jim were together, laughing and having a good time. She repeated the message that I should not worry and should enjoy myself, and Margaret added, "You've got a lot of living to do." She told me a few other things I don't recall exactly, but whatever it was sounded like what my grandmother would say. I felt she was there with Dad and I was pleased with the unexpected bonus.

When Laura said there was another Margaret trying to get through, I was stunned. It was my Aunt Margaret. The room was filled with people hoping to hear from a loved one, and for the third time I was the one receiving a message. In retrospect, it is not surprising. We have a close-knit family, and my dad, grandmother and aunt would certainly be together if possible. And they all loved to talk. But Laura said that there was something unusual about Aunt Margaret.

"The color blue surrounds her. Do you know what it is?"

I had no idea. "She has blue eyes."

She shook her head. "No, that's not it."

"Well, she had white hair, and used some kind of blue rinse to make it shiny."

"No. It's not her hair. It is all *around* her. Strange."

"She liked blue," I said.

"Maybe. But I don't think that's it." She was obviously puzzled but went on to relay more messages of support and love.

I was thrilled that they were together, and I felt protected and loved. I sent a mental message to the rest of my relatives on the other side, "If there are any more of you here, let's wait for another time. A lot of other people are waiting." Then Laura moved on, bringing messages to a half-dozen other people in the room.

Four years later, in Belleville, Illinois, for a high school reunion, I spent a day with Aunt Margaret's daughter, Barbara, and another cousin, Alice. Both of them had been close to my parents and helped them during their last years. The three of us spent the day catching up, and visiting the cemetery where our parents and other relatives are buried. It was quiet and peaceful as we walked past aged maple and oak trees, reading inscriptions on tombstones and piecing together family history we had forgotten. Barbara also talked a little about the rehabilitation her daughter, Karen, was undergoing as a result of a terrible accident four months earlier.

Toward the end of the afternoon we stopped at a small restaurant for coffee. Barbara told us more about the accident that put Karen in a wheelchair with a spinal injury. She said that the first emergency medical technician who reached Karen told her later it was a miracle he reached her so quickly. A huge traffic jam had contributed to the accident, and he had been directly across the highway when Karen's car had been hit, so he reached her immediately, instead of in the half-hour it might have taken. A few minutes later and she would have been dead. At first he thought she *was* gone, but she took one shallow breath, then, at last, another. Her car had been hit from behind, pushed under a semi and nearly flattened. Her spinal injury was the result of the severe whiplash she suffered on impact.

"Karen wasn't touched," the paramedic told Barbara. "She was in a bubble of protection, as if someone had put their arms around her to shelter her. She didn't have a drop of blood, a cut or a scratch on her."

Barbara said she believed it was her mother who had protected Karen. They had always been close, and when Margaret's vision had deteriorated and she could no longer live alone, Karen had insisted her grandmother move in with her family, and Margaret had spent her last years there.

I said, "So you *do* believe life continues after death."

"I have to," Barbara said. "I *know* it was Mom that protected Karen."

"I think so, too," I said, "partly because of something that happened a few years ago." I told them about the experience I'd had at the dowser conference, when Grandmother, Aunt Margaret and Dad visited me in spirit. My cousins listened intently and when I said we had been puzzled because Laura said Margaret had blue all around her, Barbara gasped, lurched in her chair, and her eyes filled with tears.

"Are you all right?" I asked, reaching over to steady her. *Maybe I should have kept this to myself*, I thought.

Barbara said, "That *was* Mom. I know what the blue was." She took a couple of deep breaths and continued. "You couldn't know, Marilyn, because you weren't able to be here for Mom's funeral. She absolutely loved blue. When we made the funeral arrangements I picked out a blue dress for her. Aunt Mary brought her own blue earrings from Fort Worth for Mom to wear, and the satin pillow and lining in the casket were blue. My brother almost drove the poor florist crazy, making sure all the flowers around her were blue. I don't think there were any blue flowers left in town. No wonder the psychic saw Mom surrounded by blue."

We sat in silence. How amazing that Barbara received such comfort from my experience at the conference several years earlier! I think Margaret joined Grandma and Dad that day not for me, but for Barbara. We were all impacted. Barbara's belief that her mother's spirit watches over them was strengthened; my faith in the spiritual world my mystical experiences revealed to me was validated, and Alice looked so serene when we parted, I know she also found comfort that day.

I did not mention to Barbara the dreams I'd had before the accident. Although I had no idea at the time, I am sure they were about Karen. In one dream: *My Aunt Margaret wanted me to go with her to Greece or Rome for three weeks. We would have a guide most of the time. I was badly injured.*

When someone I don't usually think about visits me in a dream, it's often a signal that something important is happening, even if I'm not aware of it until later, but I didn't spend time trying to understand this dream at the time, not even to Aunt Margaret's statement that we would have a guide, although I'd asked several times for a guide to help me on my spiritual path. On the night before Karen's accident, I had two more dreams I think were connected to it.

In the first: *I was a girl with a new job and asked my boss if I could go upstairs. When I did, I had a strong sense of déjà vu, was dizzy, and felt as if I might split from my body. I remembered I had passed out before, maybe in another life, and felt a strong desire to let myself flow, but knew I would die if I let go. I fell over, close to death. Someone called a doctor and I was taken to a hospital. I had several children, one of them still a baby. There was music playing: "Gonna Be a Heartache Tonight."*

If I gestalt the above as precognitive dreams for Karen, I would see her having a spirit guide and being hurt. She would go upstairs to the spirit world and feel that if she let go, she could die. She knew she had reincarnated before. Her children needed to be cared for. The music was surely apropos.

Later that same night I dreamed: *Dean and I were living back in St. Louis. There was a huge multi-car accident. We went inside and I told a teacher, who said no children were there at the time of the accident.*

What is most relevant about this dream is the accident occurred in St. Louis, where Karen and her family live, a teacher was involved, and none of the children were involved in the multi-car accident. In reality, Karen had been on her way to a school where she had a new teaching job, and she has three children, the youngest a baby, none of whom were with her at that time. Although the dream occurred on the morning of the accident, I didn't find out about Karen until two weeks later. She was still in a coma then, but came out of it, and improved steadily. I agree with Barbara that my aunt was watching over Karen.

FIFTEEN

six angels flew by
tilting wings in unison
to signal a right

We sometimes take the form of an angel in dreams and
OBEs because angels are not frightening to people. Most of us
know what an angel 'should' look like, and we expect them to
act in a loving, spiritual manner. An old Scottish saying, "Angels
can fly because they take themselves lightly," is a good attitude
to hold.

One night I went out of body dressed like a hippie and was
flying, looking for mountains. I saw a grassy school play-ground
surrounded by a wall, and dropped down, right into the middle
of a children's art show. I asked the artists questions and
answered theirs, then left through a side gate. Walking toward a
driveway, I flagged down a van full of young people and told the
driver if he answered a question, I would tell him a secret. He
agreed. I asked what state we were in and he said Arkansas. I
said, "My secret is I'm an angel," and flew into the air. He and
his friends were excited; they waved wildly, calling goodbye.

Next I saw two nuns deep in conversation as they walked
down the street. I dropped from the sky, landing next to them.
They didn't seem surprised. One said I had given the wrong
answer to a little girl at the art show. They had told her my
answer was wrong, and when I convinced them they were
mistaken, they wanted me to go back and tell the child. I said,
"No. What I told her was correct. It's your responsibility to tell
her. They did not want to, as she had been telling the other

children what the nuns told her. The girl was shy, with low self-esteem. The nuns were afraid that rescinding what she had said would hurt her in the eyes of the other children. I said, "Tell her to explain that she was talking with a real angel. They'll be impressed, and she won't be shy much longer."

This experience reminds me to trust what I know and to stick up for my beliefs. I was looking for mountains, or spiritual growth. The nuns represent early religious beliefs. At first, I was puzzled about being in Arkansas, but remembered that the Ozark Research Institute is there, where strong, spiritual healers teach and research energy healing.

At an angel workshop I facilitated, a number of people shared the help they have received from angels, including a woman named Cynthia. On a long car trip, she had stopped at a roadside diner for a cup of coffee. An older woman approached and asked if she could sit down. Cynthia nodded. The woman related amazing stories about her past lives that became stranger and stranger, but Cynthia listened patiently, thinking the woman obviously needed someone to talk to.

Finally Cynthia said she had to leave. As she walked to the door, the old woman cried out a warning. "Stay away from Green Valley. It's dangerous."

Cynthia thanked her, taking the words with a grain of salt. She'd never heard of Green Valley and had no idea what the woman was talking about. Hours later, hungry and tired, she pulled off the highway at a rest stop. She was about to get out of the car, when she noticed a sign—Green Valley. Without a second thought, she restarted the car and pulled away from the secluded area and back onto the road, though there was not another place to stop for many miles. The next morning she heard about a young woman's murder at the Green Valley rest stop at about the time Cynthia had been there.

"That old woman saved my life," she said. "I know she was an angel."

Another woman at the angel workshop described pulling off a highway abruptly after she heard a loud, "Stop!" from the back seat, although she was alone in the car. Brakes screeching and a loud crash sounded from around the curve ahead. She ran back to flag down oncoming cars and trucks. She said her angels have saved her more than once. The people she stopped that day must think of her as *their* guardian angel.

A man spoke of riding in a car with a friend whose eight-year-old son was asleep in the back seat. There was little traffic. Tall bushes and trees growing along the side of the road added to the tranquility of the day. The men were deep in conversation as they neared an intersection where they had the right-of-way. All of a sudden the boy sat up and shouted, "Stop, Daddy," in a panicky, loud voice. His father slammed on the brakes, coming to a halt just in time. A huge semi roared across, ignoring the traffic sign. My friend asked the child how he had known the truck was going to run the stop sign. The boy asked, "Didn't you hear the angels telling us to stop?"

Besides having angel helpers, many people find answers and support in their dreams. Clients sometimes relate quite detailed dreams to me. Often they say it's the only one they remembered having in a long time. It may carry a message they do not fully understand. We work together to decipher it.

As I began to pay more attention to dreams, intuition and synchronicity, clients, friends and family related their own extraordinary experiences to me more frequently, often preceded by, "I have never told anyone this before," or "You might think I'm crazy, but…" then describe an unusual event, such as an OBE or NDE or an especially vivid dream.

One client, Robin, had a long history of abuse, first by her mother then by her husband. She had divorced him a couple of years earlier, when she realized her life was in danger. He had removed all the doorknobs and phones from their house and threatened her with a gun. It took all her intelligence and courage to escape the destructive and frightening marriage. Shortly after the divorce, Robin had an eerie experience as she sat at the kitchen table in the apartment she shared with a friend.

Three things happened at once. Her cat yowled and raced from the room, the curtains flew straight out from the sliding screen door as if from a sharp wind, though there was no sign of a breeze before, and the pen she held in her hand began to move across the pages of the notebook on the table. She had never heard of automatic writing, the phenomena in which Spirit, or our Inner Self moves the hand in writing. When Robin looked at what she had written, she was surprised to see a reassuring, warm message from a woman whose voice she could hear as she read. She told me, "It was the voice of an angel, and I knew I was not alone." She no longer feared the future.

Despite her difficult life, she had a positive attitude and a gift for joyful living. After several months of therapy she was more confident and had begun to trust again. At our last session she said she'd had a wonderful dream she thought she understood, but she wanted my opinion. In the dream: *She was walking through lush, green woods. Flowers were abundant along the path, which was soft, yet springy and was a vibrant color that reminded her of the red dirt in Oklahoma. Ahead of her, to the right of the path, was a small shelter. She walked to it, reached inside and took out a tiny baby lamb that she held and cuddled. She awoke feeling loved and loving.*

I could see her aura expand and brighten as she related the dream to me. She said the lamb represented her belief that she could now care for and comfort herself, and could trust a new relationship. There was nothing for me to add. The next year I attended her wedding.

Another client, one who wanted to use her skills to help others, was Laurie. She was struggling to cope with a well-paying but stress-filled job as a legal assistant. She was also a massage therapist on a part-time basis, which was more fulfilling to her, but she needed an additional year in school to work as a therapist full time. It would be expensive and she thought maybe she had missed her chance. One night I had a dream I knew was for Laurie.

In the dream: *A young woman driving a car missed the right turn she wanted to make; other cars blocked the lane. At first she was upset, thinking she would be late, but she was able to turn at the next intersection. Though it took her a bit out of the way, on winding, hilly roads, she did reach her destination.*

The next time I saw Laurie, I asked if she wanted to hear a dream I thought was for her. She did, and when I finished relating it, she looked stunned. She'd had the same dream. It had impressed her so much she had drawn a picture of it, and brought it with her. She pulled a drawing from her purse —of the dream I'd had. Before that night she had almost given up her hopes of becoming a healer, thinking it was too late, but that message from her 'dream guide' helped solidify her decision to return to school. It reminded her that she could choose a new direction in her life, and that change is an option. We discussed the importance of *thinking* about what we want and *expecting* it to happen. Not long after she received a call from the school offering her a full scholarship for the year of additional training she needed. Laurie now has her own business helping others with healing massage, and she trusts that what she needs in life will be there for her.

A few months later, she told me about several incidents that illustrate the strong spiritual connection she shares with her mother, her deceased grandmothers and their mothers. One night, while she was living in the house her maternal grandmother had lived in for many years, Laurie was wakened by a loud crash. She found her grandmother's picture in the middle of the dining room floor propped up with a glass. This was the first of many events Laurie experienced in that house.

On February 4, Laurie again found her grandmother's picture propped up in the dining-room. She called her mother and they discussed its possible significance. Upon checking family records, they found that Laurie's paternal great-grandmother had died in the house on a February 4. Laurie was never frightened by these occurrences. Rather, she felt loved and protected. Her mother showed her a letter her great-grandmother had written years before, describing a visit she'd had from the spirit world. The letter was part of her legacy, and it had stipulated that it not be read or delivered until after her death. She was concerned about what people might think if they knew about her spirit visits. With Laurie's permission, I include the letter below.

On the morning of October 20, 1943, a strange thing

happened. I was in Dallas for a few weeks. I was sleeping in the northeast room or music room. Suddenly I was wide awake for no reason whatsoever. I opened my eyes and saw, coming from the corner of the room near the ceiling, next to the closet, a thick, creamy cloud, billowing like smoke, as it quickly came toward me and settled over the radio nearly directly above me. An angel appeared in the cloud, which was now white and fleecy and light blue, like clouds in the sky. This person was life size and only its head and upper body were visible. I seemed to know there were wings, however they were indistinct, except at the shoulders. She was looking directly down at me with a sad, sweet face I had never seen before. Her arms were folded over her head, clasping her hands. Her hair was wrapped around her head in braids. Or was that a crown? She was all in white. The room was in almost total darkness. I stared at the angel a few seconds or maybe a few minutes and then foolishly closed my eyes. When I opened them again, a long time afterward, she was gone.

My first impression was that God's angels do watch over us while we sleep. I'm perfectly sane, and have always been. This was not a dream or hallucination. I was as wide awake as I had ever been in my life. I've heard of angels and visions, but never believed that they were true. Now I'm convinced. My reaction to this was cold chills up and down my spine. My hair may have stood on end if it hadn't been pinned up. Tears streamed from my eyes, yet I was not afraid. Neither was I crying.

If I should tell my family or anybody of this, they would think I had lost my mind. Well I haven't. Now who was this angel? Did she have a message for me and I didn't get it, as I closed my eyes? Will this ever happen to me again? As surely as God is my judge, I'm telling the truth. I've never classed myself in a very spiritual class, but have done the best I could. This happened in Mary's home.

> Sarah Inez

An angel visited on dates that were significant to the family. Laurie's maternal great-grandmother saw the angel on the morning of October 20, 1943. She died on October 19, 1974 at the age of 100. Laurie's paternal grandmother's birthday was October 19. The letter reassured Laurie about the validity and good will of her own spirit visitors.

* * *

Once during meditation I silently asked a question of my own angel. "Who are you?" I visualized a face that looked like the sun, and thought "Sunni." I wanted to try and connect with Sunni, so I got into bed, put my hand on my chest, and asked the angel to manifest itself. My heart began to beat harder, I felt warmth pouring from my chest, and a small, glowing angel appeared directly in front of me. I asked her to take me to a place where I could learn and experience something new. She led me to a sparkling, towered city, where I was given lessons with some others, but on my return, I was frustrated at not being able to recall what we'd been taught.

When we learn something in a dream or during an OBE, it may be a lesson we received in an earlier experience that will gradually be incorporated into memory and our belief systems. Or the lesson may be even more complex.

A client, Suzanne, had a long history of conflict with her mother, but shortly before her mother died they finally began to communicate, thanks largely to Suzanne's efforts. Her mother had Alzheimer's disease, and Suzanne thought she recognized her at the end, but she wasn't sure her mother knew she loved her and forgave her for the unhappiness she had caused. Several months after her mother passed on, Suzanne dreamed she was in my second floor office.

"I walked to a window and pulled the blinds up. The night sky was studded with stars. I called out to Mother that I loved her and I wanted to know if she realized it. I asked her for a message that I would know was just for me."

Then the phone rang, waking her. Ordinarily her husband answers late night calls. But this time Suzanne sat up in bed and held out her hand. "It's for me," she said. Her husband handed her the phone. She said hello several times, but heard nothing. She hung up, certain her mother had responded to her request, and a warm rush of peace filled her. The next morning she checked their caller I.D. There was no record of the call, which did not surprise her. She said, "I don't think caller I.D. works on heavenly messages." I was to remember her dream after my own mother's passing to the spirit world.

SIXTEEN

Because I could not stop for death,
He kindly stopped for me.
The carriage held but just ourselves
And immortality. Emily Dickinson

One night I woke with music of an old World War I song still ringing in my ears. When I was a kid, Mom and I sang as we washed and dried dishes. A favorite was "How ya gonna keep 'em down on the farm, after they've seen Paree?" The week before she died I sang that song for Mom and her face lit up. By then she was unable to talk or sing, but she lifted an eyebrow and moved one shoulder in rhythm, managing a smile. She had been drifting in and out of consciousness, probably taking short visits to the other side. How could we expect her to stay here on earth when she had seen that beautiful spiritual world? As I sang that day, I tasted the salt of my tears.

The last weeks of Mom's life were bittersweet. After years of watching the steady diminishment of her bodily and cognitive functions, I felt a strange calmness. As she became unable to communicate her needs verbally, my ability to use intuition greatly increased. I talked with her about dreams, heaven, and how, when we die, we are met by others who have already passed on.

Mom's decline was a long, slow process, but in many ways she continued to be my teacher, mentor and role model. Her patience, kindness, love and wisdom continued to shine through clear blue eyes, even when she was in pain and confused.

We all reassured her that we would take care of each other;

91

that she could go on. Like many people do, Mom died when none of us were in the room. I knew she had left for a wonderful place, but I would miss her. I could picture her in the "Paris" of heaven, still sending her love to us.

The funeral service was small, with flowers, memories and prayers. I tucked a white crocheted handkerchief into the casket. Later I found that my daughter, sons, husband and brothers had each placed something with Mom, a small picture, an iris, and several other small mementos. Marguerite, who had never met Mom, but knew what a wonderful woman she was, told me she'd had a vision of Mother wearing flowered pastels, holding a very large umbrella that all her children and family were gathered under. She heard the words, "Love one another," and felt it showed our continued connection with each other through Mothers love.

Through messages in dreams, as well as physical events, our connection deepened, and has been a key to my taking that leap of faith in areas I had often resisted. Unusual and mystical events accelerated after Mom's death. I had many dreams in which Mother was young again, strong and beautiful. A number of them were precognitive, and I'll write a little more about those later.

But first I want to share something that occurred about six weeks after her death. I had gone out for a walk early one evening. I tried to meditate as I walked, but it isn't easy, as my thinking processes are always fighting to stay active. I worked at keeping a quiet mind that day. When any thoughts surfaced, I'd notice them then let go. Usually I let my mind run on, expanding the initial thought, forgetting entirely my attempt at meditation. One thought was that a good friend had written me and said after her own mother's death, she had felt her presence. I would have loved to feel Mother's presence, but did not. It popped in and out of my mind quickly. Several blocks later, when I saw a penny, I picked it up, and another thought popped in. *Why do I always find pennies? Is it because that's what I expect? What if I expected nickels or dimes?* I let the thought go, continuing my walk.

A few blocks later, I thought of a client who had called me at home earlier that day to tell me my office 'message receiver' wasn't working. After her call, I had corrected the problem with my telephone answering machine. The mental flash I had while walking was the dream she'd told me about, in which she received a message from her deceased mother.

The brief recall of her dream reminded me that I wanted a message from my mother. Maybe my personal 'message receiver' wasn't turned on. I believe in life after death and knew that Mom was happy and well, but I missed her. I thought, *Mom you know I love you, but I would like some message from you. It doesn't have to be big.* Then I thought about expecting to find pennies, rather than something more valuable and thought, *Mom, I would like something big, something wonderful and amazing, a specific, out-of-the-ordinary event—a Christmas present really, a surprise. No rush.* Then, I thought, *Actually, if you are going to do something, let's not wait around. I'd like a message very soon.* That felt right. *One more thing. Tell Dad I love him too.*

By this time I was nearly home. I walked faster, feeling light and positive. As soon as I was inside, I kicked off my shoes and went into the kitchen to get a glass of water and see if I could help with the dinner my husband had started. The phone rang. Dean answered and said it was for me. It was the publisher of Papier-Mache Press.

I was shocked. Ever since I'd begun writing poetry, I had dreamed of having a poem published in one of their anthologies, which focused on women and aging. They received thousands of submissions for each book, and though some of my poems had been held for consideration in the past, the odds weren't great that they'd ever find one of my poems right for them. The last ones I'd sent had been returned with a very nice rejection letter.

Now the publisher was on the phone. I could hardly hear her. Either I was too excited or we didn't have a great connection, but I *could* hear her say they'd like my permission to use one of my poems for their new book, Generation to Generation. I blurted out my acceptance immediately, with no idea which poem they wanted. She was telling me the terms of the contract and my mind was blank. The terms didn't matter to me. I was thrilled. When I finally asked her which poem they'd chosen, she named one I did not remember sending. I'm sure I sounded surprised.

She said, "I picked this one because I like it a lot. It is sweet, it made me smile and I know my father will love it." The poem was *Senior Golfer*. Hanging up, I rushed back into the kitchen to tell Dean about the call.

"That is amazing! What a perfect Christmas gift," he said, on hearing my news. "Isn't it sort of unusual though, kind of odd, for them to be working so late on Friday, less than a week before Christmas?

His words shook me. They were almost the exact words I had used, just minutes earlier, when asking my mother to send me a message. Why hadn't I realized this immediately, the moment I took the call? I went into another room, wrote out exactly what I had thought and asked for during my walk then handed the paper to Dean. He read it, nodded, and said, "Your Mom always did know what you really wanted."

Does that mean that Mother had figured out a way for my poem to be accepted at the moment I asked? I have no idea, but when I find such wonderful serendipity, I wonder. Coincidences can be arranged very lovingly. When I "put things out to the universe," as Marguerite says, things happen, and more and more often it is happening quickly, sometimes instantaneously.

The next day during my walk, as I approached the spot where I'd asked Mom for a message I thought it would be nice to get another sign, even a small one, that she was still with us, though in a different dimension. I noticed something shiny on the street. A dime. And a nickel. Then I saw several more! I remembered wanting to find more than pennies the day before. Was this a coincidence? Is it a coincidence that when we think of someone we want to talk with, before we can dial the number, the phone rings and it is that person? When it happens again and again and again?

It's important to ask for what you want clearly, then to let it go. The first time I consciously did this was also during a walk.

My private practice had slowed down and I had enjoyed extra time to do things at home, to relax, to write, but now I felt a desire to increase the number of clients I saw. I clearly asked for more business and when I got home and checked my phone messages, there were two calls from potential clients. Over the next couple of weeks, my schedule became more crowded and it continued growing, until I consciously asked my angels to slow it down a little.

I have quit worrying about whether I'll have enough time to do things I want or whether I will have enough income. When I want or need a change, I "throw my request out to the universe," and things change. Now, when I have an appointment at a time that, for one reason or another, is not convenient, I invariably get a call requesting a change. Then I'll get another call from someone else, until finally my schedule fits my needs that day just perfectly.

Does this mean we can always wish for, or ask for something and get it immediately? No, but more often than not, if we are in a positive emotional and spiritual place in our lives, we receive help from our angels. The help may not always be in a form we can understand right away, so trust to the goodness of intention and move on.

SEVENTEEN

Earthbound—Holding the Vision

Belief will move mountains they say
and we create our own reality.
And I stand, one foot planted firmly
on either side of belief.
I want to fly. I want to believe.
I want to believe I can fly
but I've seen so many crumpled bodies
lying at the foot of the mountain.
I want to fly...
but I believe I can walk.

The question of what happens to us after death has been argued for generations. Even those who believe our soul continues look for proof or understanding. People who have had near-death experiences (NDEs) don't always agree with each other. For some, the experience of leaving the body, then returning, has had a negative effect, especially when they are met with ridicule or derision. One woman told me of a near-death experience she had more than twenty years earlier. When she had tried to tell her mother, right after it happened, her mother stopped her, saying, "Don't tell anyone. They'll think you're crazy. Forget it." She kept silent for years, carrying feelings of shame, until she came across an article about NDEs. She was quite relieved to find that hers was not an uncommon experience.

Several years ago a friend of mine, Claudia, became ill,

collapsed and stopped breathing. When we talked about it later, she said she had soul-traveled across water, toward beautiful, snow-covered mountains. At the time, her daughter, Katie, was on a mountain in Colorado hundreds of miles away. Katie later told her mother she *felt* her spirit pass through her; that it felt like icy prickles rushing through her body. Even though Katie had not known of Claudia's illness before, she was certain the spirit she felt had been her mother. She immediately raced down the mountain to call home. Fortunately the EMTs were able to revive her Claudia.

I experienced a physical sensation similar to the one Katie described. It was when a client was telling me about her deceased husband. She'd had several dreams in which he had given her help or advice, and she had often felt his presence, which comforted her. As she talked, I had the distinct sensation of being filled with a tingly presence, as if icy crystals had instantaneously filled my body. It was unlike anything I had ever felt before, and the hair on my arms and the back of my neck rose. I felt deep satisfaction that those who have passed on can still communicate with and support their loved ones.

In the year after Mom passed on, my dreams increased in their intensity and were emotionally laden. If our dreams are part of connection with spirit and other dimensions as I believe, then I was being pulled more and more into those dimensions, while my 'physical world' remained as busy as ever. My dreams were filled with metaphors and symbolism that gave me assurance Mother continued on another plane. A perplexing dream became clear to me several weeks after it happened.

My parents had been visiting, and were packing to fly home. They were running late. Dad did not seem concerned, which was unusual. Mom, still in her slip, was fixing her hair in the bathroom. I was afraid they would miss their plane, and offered to pack Mom's things. She said that would be nice. There were three small, stuffed animals in her suitcase. I asked about them and she said to leave them in. "It was a mistake," she said. "They are going somewhere else."

A week later, when my daughter told me she was pregnant, I

wanted to think that the dream was a precognitive message she was going to have a baby. When she had a miscarriage, I knew the dream had been sending a different message, one to prepare me emotionally for the disappointing news, so I could help my daughter.

Another dream toward the end of that year held particular significance for me. In it: *Dean, my brother, John, and I were going home after a church service. I was walking ahead of them, on white sand, and I looked back. A large egg had fallen to the ground from a tree and cracked. John rushed to help a baby bird that was trying to break out of the shell. It fluttered around a bit then flew away.*

Besides reminding me of the cycle of death and rebirth, I thought about my own children 'flying away' as they were older and of my own metamorphosis as my life changes. In another dream I attempted to explain a different concept of time. *I was talking with a client about worry and hope. I asked if she believed time is relative, as Einstein did. "For instance, we've already lived 10 years from now—and my youngest son is grown, has a good job. He is married and doing well. Now, we are back in the present time, when he's younger. But we don't need to worry about him. We're not predicting the future—we already know it because we live the past, future, and present all at once."*

This dream suggests a possible reason for the déjà vu experience. Although we dream every night, most of us re-member little of what occurs in them, but many remain in our subconscious. Then, when something happens that we have dreamed about, we have a dim recollection of the incident, yet don't know where the memory came from. I'm fascinated with theories about time and have had several other dreams or OBEs in which someone is explaining a theory to me, or I'm explaining it to someone else. Dreams that occur at special times, like the end of the year, always get my attention.

On December 30 that year I dreamed: *I was at a big family gathering at my parent's house. My grandmother said she just wanted her life back to be able to do small things like washing the dishes or sewing, and to tell the children about the miracles.*

I hoped to hear more about the miracles, but woke up before I could ask Grandma about them. Since we are all at different places in our learning and growth, our needs are different.   I

***

When I read The Messengers, a depiction of Nick Bunick's experiences in a past life as St. Paul, I was struck by Bunick's statement that during a past life regression he saw Jesus become angry with the priests. They had set up an artificial barrier when they insisted people communicate with God only through them. He said Jesus told us we should speak to God directly, that we have the ability within ourselves, and don't need others to talk for us. We can learn from others and enjoy the exhilaration of singing and praying in a group, but we do have a direct line to God. I was further reminded of inward trusting when I read Edgar Casey's caveat about psychics. He said we can receive information from psychics but our best information comes from our inner spirit and we can increase our access to it through practice.

In January, two months after Mom died, I dreamed:

I was in the backyard of my childhood home. Mom was standing by the flower bed by the fence. The grass had begun greening, but the borders were messy. I wanted to help Mom, and started to trim the grass around the vegetable and flower beds, using a mower-edger that was so powerful it dragged me around the yard. I hung on desperately, but accidentally cut a huge kohl rabi open. (Mom and Dad always grew some just for me). There was something alive inside—a white, hairless creature, like a very ugly baby with huge, round eyes. I turned away. I did not want to see it. I walked toward Mom, feeling bad because I had ruined the unusual vegetable, but Mother was smiling and unconcerned. We walked around the side of the house and Mom knelt on the grass, pushed green fronds aside and discovered beautiful flowers in brilliant hues. Her face glowed with delight. She called, "Marilyn, look!" I realized I was dreaming and Mom was showing me her beautiful new garden. Flowers were springing up all around her.

When I woke, I felt peaceful and happy, with the certainty that she was not gone, but tending flowers in a different garden. She was never happier than when she was nurturing plants, flowers, or her family. I thanked Mother for her message of love.

Raymond Moody, the author of Life After Life and other books about our continued existence *after* this life on earth, writes that when you dream of someone who has departed this world, it is quite likely a visit from that person. He cited numerous instances in which people received not only comfort, but specific messages that only the deceased person could have sent.

A week later, just before falling asleep, I had a vision in which I saw, as if through a camera lens held high above, my brother Jim and me when we were two and three years old. One after another, with the motion of a zoom lens, black and white photos of Jim and me as children, then teenagers, came into focus. The last pictures, in color, were as we look now. My parents still see us, but from a different dimension, from a distance. Circumstances change after death, but we do not cease to exist, nor does our connection with those we love end.

On another night I felt intense vibration and a sense of being filled with energy and light. I was drawn into the light of love, God and ecstasy. Then I had a series of dreams about my life path. In one: *I was following someone else and got bogged down in mud.* I thought of my red bird dream and wondered if I'd been getting stuck lately following the paths of others.

I woke up missing my mother then I felt a gentle hand on my back. It was Mom, soothing me. I relaxed, fell asleep, and woke in a lucid dream. *I was at a party, and began to fly. I noticed several old coins on top of a cabinet, and thought they might be valuable. Flying out the front door and across the lawn I flew over the edge of a cliff. I knew I was OK since I was in my dream body. Mountains rose in the distance. There were Indian symbols in the sky and I heard an explosion, probably a ritual. I alternated flying and floating down, spinning, enjoying myself, singing, "I don't want to set the world on fire."*

Even after years of OBEs and lucid dreams, I was still surprised, usually pleasantly, when some new phenomena such

101

as chimes occurred when I shifted consciousness. One warm spring night I stayed in the guest room at Marguerite's house. She told me there was good spirit energy in the guest room. I stayed up awhile reading in bed before deciding to call it a night. I closed my eyes and immediately heard musical chimes on an ascending note. They woke me to another dimension, and I flew out of body.

Later that night I drifted into a dream. *At an all-girls' school, my granddaughter and several other students were sitting outdoors along a walkway in some sort of modules. Gershwin's 'Rhapsody in Blue' was playing as I strolled toward the parking lot, appreciating the day and enjoying the music, thinking that the girls were lucky to be students there. They seemed happy and it was clear they loved the music, too. It was an exhilarating day.*

About a month later I visited Marguerite again. When I went to bed that night, I felt a refreshing breeze coming in through the window. The shade was up and the light of a full moon brought faint illumination into the room. I read for a few minutes, before turning off the bedside lamp. Almost immediately I felt a gentle touch on my legs and back, as if from a caring spirit. When it stopped, I got up to close the window, as it had started to rain. Closing my eyes again, I felt vibrations for a minute then drifted off to sleep. I woke up hearing the sound of Marlene Dietrich singing *Falling in Love Again* playing in my head.

I had no idea at the time what the following 'music' dream meant, though I suspect it was a precognitive experience about an incident I write about in chapter twenty. In the dream: *Garth Brooks was sitting on the edge of the stage, auditioning for me, playing his guitar and singing a song, "A Stranger Came," a song I'd never heard before.*

I asked friends who are country-western music lovers, but no one I asked ever heard of the song. My guess is it has not been written yet. Many composers are said to hear or receive their music in dreams, including Mozart and Billy Joel. Writers, inventors, and scientists like Albert Einstein have spoken of receiving ideas in dreams.

EIGHTEEN

The really valuable method of thought to arrive at a logically coherent system is intuition. Albert Einstein

An example of family ties is an experience I'm sure my husband will never forget. It occurred shortly after my father died. Dean woke abruptly in the middle of the night, sat up in bed and saw the spirit of my father standing at the foot of the bed.

Dad said, "Dean, if you quit smoking, you'll enjoy your seventies."

My husband was 60 at the time and he took the message seriously. That night he decided to quit, and within a year he stopped a smoking habit of over forty years. It is one thing to receive messages from our spirits, guides or angels and quite another to follow through on the suggestions and insights they give us.

***

The summer after Mother's death, my family met in Colorado for a week. It was reassuring to know that when we got home everything would be as it was when we left. In the past, we had returned from trips to find plants and flowers dead and the foundation of the house damaged from drought, or food spoiled because the electricity had gone off or a freezer door had been left ajar. Hiring a neighbor boy to water had not been enough to prevent damage. Texas is tough in the summer when the temperature hits a hundred degrees for weeks on end. It plays havoc with our yards and gardens.

This time, a young college student house-sat for us. She

lived with her parents and worked full time, hoping to be able to afford her own place someday. Priscilla liked taking care of friends' houses occasionally, enjoying the quiet it afforded her. We knew she would take good care of our garden, and would work to keep even one petunia from 'biting the dust.' She seemed delighted with our guest room, which is furnished with the bedroom suite Mom and Dad bought when they married, in 1934. Besides the blue and white quilt Mom had given us, the room was filled with old and new family pictures. We told Priscilla to feel free to use any room in the house—to read, play music and enjoy herself.

We had a wonderful, worry-free vacation, and when we drove back felt rested. As we neared our house, we noticed how lush and green the yard was. Priscilla must have watered the grass and flowers every day. She told us everything had gone fine, though she'd locked herself out of the house accidentally one day then had to climb over shrubs and air conditioner through an un-locked window into the garage.

I was glad Priscilla did not have to rush off. I felt there was something she wanted to tell us. There was.

She said, "I don't want to intrude, but do you know there is a ghost in the house?"

Dean said, "That is probably Marilyn's mother."

We assured her she wasn't intruding on our personal space, and were interested in hearing what had happened. After she told us what her week had been like, I asked her to write it down. The following are excerpts from her note.

...I had an incredibly relaxing time. I suppose this is a—if not the—key to my experience. There truly is something to be said in the difference. First of all, I had the overwhelming sense that I was secure and there was nothing to fear....As I put my things away in your guest room I felt a strong presence. It was in the pictures, the dresser, the bed. Initially I avoided being in there at all. I slept on the couch with the TV on all night for background noise. I avoided silence—quite the opposite of my usual desires. I woke on the third or fourth night and the tele-vision was off. I hadn't turned it off. I felt uneasy, but decided

not to worry about it. I was going back to sleep when I saw and felt a light. An inexplicable glow that wrapped around me like a flannel blanket. Like a warm cloud. Very strange I admit. I felt as though your couch was, quite literally, holding me. I remember smiling and drifting back to sleep peacefully. I felt as if I was being protected, loved, cared for. Just for being me. Just for being alive.

Marilyn, I know you and your family grieve the loss of your mother. I wish I had known her before. All I can say is, she is with you. She is still here. The change is that there is no hindrance. Nothing stopping her—not age, not disease. If 'glow' was a color, if it were soft light with yellow and blue, all colors, yet not one particular one, your mother would bear the name. There is more. I was on the porch and the garage light was turned off...I did not see the switch being flipped but I did see the light go out. I thought a bulb might have burned out, but when I went in, I looked at the switch that had been up only minutes before. I had looked at it specifically before going out to make sure it was well lit. I took a deep breath and turned the light back on. As I did so, I felt warmth—and an energy—as if when I flipped the switch it was merely a game of fun. I smiled as I realized I was meant to be there. Initially I felt as though I had intruded upon a deeply personal family thing. Yet that glow, that warmth takes the doubt away and dismisses it. Sends it so far away I no longer ask why, or is this feeling directed at me? I don't doubt that it is anymore. I know it is. All I can say is thank you for the opportunity to experience such a feeling. I will house sit anytime! Thanks for listening. Priscilla

Not only did I appreciate her willingness to share her experiences with us, but it was especially warming to read her beautiful words, her poetic way of expressing her affirmation of Mother's presence in spirit.

Pricilla, Dean and I aren't the only ones Mom has visited. Our daughter, Susan, has felt her presence on more than one occasion. Once, when she was feeling discouraged with the lack of progress being made in remodeling her home, she sensed Mother's presence and heard her voice say, with a note of joyful anticipation, "Isn't this an adventure!"

Susan felt better immediately and said, "Yes, it is."

Soon after, when a new friend of hers came over to lend a hand with painting, he noticed a photograph of Mother. He asked, "Who's that?"

"My grandmother," Susan said.

"She's here, you know," he said.

"Yes. I know."

NINETEEN

When asked, "What is the purpose of life?"
by writer William Elliott, his Holiness,
the Dalai Lama responded, "Happiness."
From Tying Rocks to Clouds

Soon after those experiences I had several vivid dreams that expressed my reluctance to expose my inner self. In one: *I was a teen-age girl, at home alone. I stepped outside onto barren, yellow ground, walked fifty yards from the house and saw several girls coming toward me. One of them called, "Hey, come here," in a hostile voice. I was scared, and wanted to run back inside, but I had dropped my purse, with wallet inside, and it lay on the ground between us. I felt helpless and angry, and wished I had paid more attention before coming out.* The dream symbolically reflected fear of losing my identity (purse and wallet) and exposing myself to possible danger by 'coming out,' revealing spiritual changes in my life.

Later, *I dreamed a man called me about my book, saying there was a 'call' for poems and stories.* As a child, I learned some people have callings to be priests or nuns. I had not known we could have a calling for a different life work.

The following dream supported my decision to stop hiding my beliefs and experiences: *Uncurtained windows and glass sliding doors covered a wall next to a walk-in closet in my new house. People could see inside, so I was getting dressed in the closet. A friend and her husband pushed open the sliding door. I said, "Wait. I'm changing clothes." She said she had come to get help from me. I said I'd help after I finished dressing.*

I woke up before I found out what her problem was, but as in most dreams, the problem was really the dreamer's—mine.

I had agreed to do a workshop at a weekend retreat. I was going to 'come out of the closet' about my OBEs and other mystical events in my life. The dream affirmed my decision. My friend and her husband, attractive people who are careful with appearance, represent my need to 'look good' to others. I had been concerned about other people's reactions. The workmen in the dream were slow getting their job done, and I knew I was dragging my feet with my spiritual work.

The focus of the retreat was personal change in the new millennium. The main speaker was an excellent facilitator and the weekend was filled with opportunity for personal growth and learning. The retreat was set in a tranquil, wooded area behind green lawns; it bordered a clear, flowing river. The cabins were large, light and airy, with sturdy, comfortable beds.

After unpacking my bags, I was going to run down to the main building, but the cool breeze coming through the open windows was relaxing. I decided to start the weekend by taking time to absorb the spiritual and positive feelings here. I stretched out on the bed, closed my eyes and drifted off for about ten minutes, until wakened by a gentle, cradle-like rocking, I lay there for several moments, feeling welcomed, then opened my eyes. The rocking slowed, stopped. I got up, and tried to push the bed in the rocking motion, but it didn't budge. I felt that the sensation of rocking was a welcome from the spirits.

I was excited to be at the retreat but a little nervous about my workshop. I had taught college classes, given numerous talks and facilitated many groups, but this would be different. Most of those attending were long-term members of A.R.E.

My three-hour presentation was scheduled for the next day. Several sessions would be held simultaneously and I didn't know which concerned me most, the fear no one would sign up for my workshop, or that a lot of people would sign up. I was concerned that what I had planned might be either too strange or too elementary. I had put together handouts, written copious notes and reviewed them several times. I planned on group participation, but if I used all my materials, with group input, it could have been an all day workshop. Luckily, I misplaced my notes and handouts. There was no brown folder to be seen. I decided there must be a reason I had misplaced it. I knew what I wanted to get across, and if I forgot part of it, so what! My notes were just a security blanket.

My workshop was titled "Toto! We're Not in Kansas Anymore!" The premise was that we create spiritual connections through dreams and other altered states of consciousness. I referred to the novel, Flatland, by Edwin Abbott, who used geometric figures to show how dimensions can exist which we do not perceive. It shows the difficulty we might have in accepting them. I recommend it for anyone struggling with the concept of multiple dimensions. You don't have to be a math whiz to enjoy and learn from this book.

One way to understand paranormal experiences is to think about color and sound vibrations and how we are able, with our limited five senses, to access only part of the spectrum. Dogs hear sounds we cannot, but we know those sounds exist. We learn to connect with other spiritual dimensions by paying attention to our dreams, our intuition, to extrasensory perceptions, spiritual experiences and altered states of consciousness such as those reached in near-death-experiences and OBEs, as well as through meditation, prayer and chanting.

During the workshop, I shared some of my experiences and encouraged others to share theirs. Most of the participants were eager to discuss paranormal and spiritual events in their lives.

Rita told about her work in a healing prayer group. She uses meditation, and prays for whoever needs healing, even a person she doesn't know. During one healing meditation, she envisioned a beautiful sky, so unique it was etched in her memory. Sometime later she was introduced to a woman who said she had already met Rita when she was in the hospital with what she had been told was an incurable illness. One day she was alone in her room. Two spirits came in, operated on her and healed her. She said one of the 'spirits,' a nurse, was Rita.

The woman's doctor couldn't explain how she had been

cured, but said it was not the first time he'd heard such a story. The woman told Rita that during the healing she had looked out the window and the colors in the sky were incredible. Afterward, she fumbled in her bedside drawer for a camera her daughter had left. She took a picture of the clouds and swirls of color and carries the picture with her. She showed it to Rita; it was the view Rita had seen in her visualization. Even though Rita had believed in healing meditation and prayer, this experience shocked her. She realized she no longer *believed*—she *knew*!

Those are the same words Raymond Moody used at a lecture about his book, <u>Reunion</u>. He had constructed a psychomanteum in an attempt to replicate the one he had seen in caves in Greece. This was a darkened room, used in ancient times, in which people could see and talk with loved ones who had passed into spirit. In the center of the underground room was a huge copper vat filled with water, so the reflection could call spirits.

Moody used a room with its walls covered in black velvet. A mirror was on one wall. Participants sat on a chair so low that they could not see their reflection in the mirror. The only light was a very low watt bulb behind them. Graduate students who were part of a study Moody conducted, described their experiences seeing and/or talking with a deceased loved one. Moody believed them, but when his own departed grandmother came into his well-lit living room and talked with him, it shocked him. His world view shifted. He no longer believed—he *knew*.

At the time an unusual or paranormal experience occurs, I *know* it's real, but later, if the event doesn't fit my previous belief system, I still use self-talk that shores up old doubts. Cognitive dissonance is stressful, and my lifetime of traditional beliefs can overshadow my own experiences. I used to think I didn't take my old beliefs so seriously, and that I was open to new ideas, but shifting to a new view is harder than I expected. It helps to be around others who are exploring their spiritual paths; it is discouraging to be met with skepticism when we still doubt ourselves.

✳✳✳

Some of us are in tune with our unconscious and superconscious and spiritual knowing through our dreams; others are clairvoyant—know what another person is thinking, or have the ability to know future events, or they see or hear messages from angels or spirits. Edgar Casey, who lived from 1877 to 1945, had the ability to go into a trance and 'read' a person's medical problems through the Akashic records. He would then suggest remedies, and even where those remedies could be found. His track record for accuracy was amazing.

Many spiritual healers, like Elizabeth Weedn and Gladys McCoy of the Ozark Research Institute, work with auras and healing energy to heal, both 'hands on' and from a distance. They say we can all do this. It is a skill we may have long neglected, but it is becoming accessible to more of us as we tune in to our spiritual selves.

Not long after the retreat, I had a number of dreams about people who wanted change in their lives. They would call me on the phone for help. I was still ambivalent about speaking about spiritual events in my life. I don't like conflict or controversy, even though I know resolving it, dealing with it, can help one grow. Speaking at the retreat had been wonderful, but what about sharing my story with others who are not so receptive?

TWENTY

Truth ... once seen and spoken, can no longer be
denied in our hearts, no matter how fiercely we try to pretend
that life is what we once were told.

As November 10, the anniversary of my mother's death
approached, I felt I should do *something* but didn't know what.
I decided to just be open to my intuition. On the ninth I dreamed:
*a tornado was coming. I warned my family and neighbors. We
took shelter, and nobody was hurt.* The dream represented my
dread of the storm of my own emotions. I still felt a gray cloud
of sadness hovering over me. Then I woke the morning of
November 10 with a dream that lifted the cloud from my heart:

*I was visiting Mom in a nursing home. She was old, in a
wheelchair, but was sitting up straight, smiling. She asked if I
thought it would be all right if she went to an AA meeting there.
She said, "Even though I don't drink, maybe I could be helpful.
What do you think?" I knew one of the saddest results of the
strokes she'd suffered was that they left her unable to help others.
I said they would be happy to have her there. When I looked for
her later so I could say goodbye I found her sitting in a large
group. They began to sing and she waved to me as if to say, "Go
on, I'm fine." I waved back and left.*

This dream had a profound affect on my emotional well-
being, reminding me Mom didn't need me any more to take care
of her. From that day on I felt lighter. The cloud had lifted.

I had another tornado dream, one where no one was hurt then
I dreamed that when I had trouble with the bike I was riding
through a tunnel, I fixed it myself and said I needed to get home

to my daughter. Looking at riding the bike metaphorically, I'm proceeding on my life path. I rode through the tunnel, a symbol of transition between dimensions, after being stuck emotionally because of my grief over Mom's death. In going home to my daughter, I was ready to return my focus on the living. My spiritual and emotional lives were in the process of transition. A dream I had soon after offered further illumination and guidance:

I was cleaning out closets, putting my parents' clothes into plastic bags to donate to charity. I noticed a tiny gold pin on Dad's suit and a jeweled pin on one of Mom's dresses. I held up a dress and thought it would fit me. Maybe I could wear some of the clothes. I got out baking soda to clean the vaporizer, amazed at how many layers of residue coated the inside.

Though Mom and Dad have both moved on to the spirit dimension, parts of them are within me, which pleases me. Cleaning the encrusted layers from the vaporizer represents clearing unneeded emotional residue from past lives as well as the present one.

A psychic once told me I'd spent an entire past life helping slaves escape to the north through the Underground Railroad. He explained how helping others was residue I carried over to my present life—it seems so natural I never question it. In my dream there were many layers of residue blocking a good flow. I'm trying to raise my awareness of old habits and beliefs, to rethink them, 'scrubbing' them from my life if they no longer contribute to my growth. Like a vaporizer converting water into stream, I can convert my beliefs or release them.

One night I went to bed, began to feel anxious, and asked for help to become calm. I felt gentle patting on my back for some time, as if my mother was there. I relaxed, slept and my dreams were peaceful. On another night, I asked for an angel or guide, and went out-of-body. I followed a light into the stars and then to a cave-like place where several women were gathered in a circle, praying. One of them was my mother, but I could not see her clearly. She said 'Eleanor' was just one of many lives we had shared, and that we would be together again, but not as Eleanor and Marilyn.

One night while visiting Marguerite, I went to bed late, closed my eyes, and after a few deep breaths, heard the sound of chimes that I had first heard there. I flew up, into the sky and heard a woman singing. Later I fell into sleep and had a vivid dream: *I climbed a huge tree to the top, which was like a floor I could walk on. At the far edge of the tree a branch stuck up through the floor. I began to walk toward it, and the tree started to tilt. I did not want to fall on my face or kill myself. I could go back to the other side of the tree and not fall at all.*

A tree represents spiritual growth. In this dream I had reached a plateau and could move on, but was afraid I might fall. I considered backing down from the position I'd already reached. When I was growing up I loved to climb trees. My brother and I would climb to the highest branches we could, hang on a limb then leap to another, held up only by the air and momentum for brief moments. Looking back, it was probably dangerous, but we were not afraid.

When I was about ten, and had climbed high in the maple tree across our street, my mother came out onto the porch. I called to her, and when I was sure she was watching, I leapt for another branch of the tree. She waved to me, smiled then went back into the house. Years later she told me I'd nearly scared her to death, but she didn't want me to be afraid. When I'm fearful now, it helps to think of the encouragement my parents gave me. I know they still help, and send grace from the spirit world.

***

I had asked for a guide to help me move forward spiritually. I loved feeling Mom and Dad's presence, but I didn't want to hold them near earth if they were ready to move on. Then I had an unexpected and frightening experience. About midnight one December night I went to bed in the guest room. Dean was asleep at the other end of the house. We had both coughed and wheezed the night before, keeping each other awake. I checked to be sure the doors were locked. Only a dim glow from a bathroom nightlight kept the room from total darkness when I turned off the bedside lamp. I felt uneasy right away. An odd turbulence stirred in the air above the bed, *inside the bedroom,* like roiling clouds before a storm. *What is that?* I thought. My body tightened with anxiety.

Looking to my left, I was shocked to see a long-haired, bearded man, his face in profile, sitting or kneeling next to the bed. A spirit! I was frightened. Attempting to find out if he was a good spirit, I asked "Did Jesus send you here?"

When he said no, I panicked. I screamed in my mind, "Help! I need help! At once I heard a click, as if a lamp had been turned on, and ambient light filtered into the room. I thought Dean must have wakened and gone into the den. I called, "Dean!" as loud as I could. No answer. But the spirit had disappeared.

Feeling slightly braver, I got up and rushed to the den. No sign of Dean. The lamp was on. I sat in the chair next to it, and felt my mother's presence. A few minutes later, leaving the light on, I walked to the other end of the house. Dean was sound asleep. I jumped into bed, not caring if we both coughed all night. I was calm, filled with peace. My request for help had been answered. Then I remembered the click of the porch light (page 105). It's true that we are not alone. Feeling a little like Scarlett O'Hara, I said to myself, "I'll think about it tomorrow," and drifted off to sleep.

I realized later that the spirit who came might have been a loving one, even if not sent specifically from Jesus. In fact, I *had* asked for a guide several days earlier, and the spirit had seemed non-threatening, with a quiet voice, but I had not expected anyone to actually appear in my room. Was the song Garth Brooks sang in my earlier dream, 'And a Stranger Came,' a precognitive message I ignored? I realize I could have risked further communication. There was no need to panic.

I sometimes use that memory when I'm confronted with fear of the unknown, or when I feel I have been turned loose on an adventure without a book of instructions.

TWENTY ONE

Imagination
What if you slept?
And what if, in your sleep you dreamed?
And what if, in your dream
you went to heaven
and there plucked
a strange and beautiful flower?
And what if, when you awoke,
you had the flower in your hand?
Samuel Taylor Coleridge

On January 1, a few days after my unexpected visit from the spirit, I went out-of-body in the form of an angel. I was flying, and carrying a little girl in my arms, helping people who had died. I would call to them, and point toward the light. Some were unhappy and fearful. One boy wanted to go back because he missed his parents. I told him he would be surprised some day when old friends showed up—that he'd be glad to see them. Meanwhile, there were lots of new friends for him to make.

I had led a number of spirits to a waiting area and was ready to go back. The little girl wanted to come with me. She could not fly alone, so I reached out, took her hand, and carried her. She wasn't a spirit yet. Then her life force began to spill out of her mouth until there was none left. She was dead. We were in a long tunnel. Workmen there turned to look at us, and one man asked what he could do. The girl was completely limp. She had to be taken to the way-station and I left her with the man, knowing he was there for that reason. She was safe. She was not alone. It was time for me to return to my present life on earth.

In another OBE, I flew through the night sky surrounded by stars; then I was on a mountain, clutching at the crumbly dirt, climbing, so I could see what was on the other side. At the top, I looked out on a valley and another, higher mountain, where people climbed toward its mesa-like top. Remembering I was not in my body, so did not need to struggle with climbing, I flew to the top, where a number of people were gathered. Some were standing in a line; others milled around aimlessly. They had died, and some of them seemed to be aware of it. Others were puzzled.

A young, blond woman looked worried. I knew she had small children and when I told her not to be concerned, that her family was all right, she was relieved. It was true, but I wondered *how* I knew it. I thought about home, and was back in bed immediately. At no time was I afraid. When traveling out-of-body I am almost never frightened. Fear resides only in the body I leave behind.

These experiences led me to question myself about the reason I had been given this gift of traveling out of body. I felt there might be some purpose other than having an interesting time, or answering my curiosity. One night, after my prayers, I offered to do something helpful. Instantly I flew out of body into the night sky then gently 'dropped down' into the battle zone of a war. The soldiers wore what looked like World War I uniforms. For a moment I thought I was a soldier, part of the battle, but then I remembered I was a spirit, with no reason to fear for myself. Many men were being slaughtered. After they were shot and killed, they would step out of their bodies, then look around, confused. I waved, called them over and directed them toward a path on the right side of a road. Without a question the first soldiers started walking; others followed. A wall ran along the right side of the path, concealing what was behind it. After about a hundred yards, the path ended and the soldiers would turn to the right, out of sight. Somehow I knew they would be shown the next steps by someone else.

A small frame house sat at the edge of the field. Two little girls were walking up the steps to the porch. A voice told me to show them the path, too. The children wanted to go back into the house, but I got them to come to me, then handed the younger child a little doll that I picked from the air. The other girl had a stuffed animal. I told them to hurry, and catch up with the soldiers.

They asked if they had died, and I said, "Yes, and now you're going to heaven." In response to another question, I said, "No, I'm not dead. I'm an angel."

I thought it would confuse them if I said I wasn't quite sure who I was at the moment. I only knew that I was there to do this work and felt I had done it before many times. When they were safely on the path, I returned home. I could only travel so far.

Before that night I hadn't realized that some people need help moving on to the next dimension after death. Since then I have found that the Monroe Institute in Virginia teaches people who have OBEs how to do this work. It's a new concept for me, but so are the spiritual and energy healings I've witnessed. I suspect part of my life lesson is to accept life's mysteries with that leap of faith I used to find so hard.

My dreams and out-of-body-experiences had shifted from play and exploration to more serious ventures. Besides wanting to understand their purpose, I desired clarity about the direction my spiritual path should take. My thoughts and feelings bounced back and forth. I looked back at the dreams in my journal and decided to pay special attention to my dreams that week. Several of them pointed toward teaching and writing about spiritual experiences. I was already writing, but with several projects in process I was torn between which to focus on. I wanted to finish something. I asked for a dream to help me decide.

A young boy was brought to me for help writing a paper. I told him to use a recorder to tape his thoughts, then write what he had recorded. The dream felt like encouragement to write my own experiences.

In another dream: *We had just moved into a huge house with many servants. One went outside to look at the garden, which was all dried out. She said, "Surely you can find someone to take care of all this. When much is given, we must take care of those things, whether material or spiritual."*

The dream was another reminder that our talents and gifts should be used and nurtured.

One night I asked for help or information from a benevolent and wise spirit. I had a lucid dream in which:

I ran around the side of my childhood home toward the front yard, feeling a tremendous joy of anticipation. A car was parked in front of our next door neighbor's house. I couldn't see who was in it because a large bush blocked my view, but I knew someone special was there. I jumped onto the hood of the car to look in. Dad sat in the driver's seat, with Mom in the back. Dad gave me advice about doing what makes me happy.

Then I dreamed: *My friend Susie and I were on a trip and were lost. Empty bird nests were in trees lining a sidewalk. I said, "Don't worry. There aren't any birds here, so they must have all learned to fly."* Like a mama bird, all my children are grown and have 'flown the nest.' I sometimes worried about them. I think the dream was a reminder they are quite capable of getting through whatever circumstances life hands them.

At the end of the month, I visited my son, Robert. He had just moved into a furnished house he rented while its husband and wife owners were in Europe. Both artists, their soul-filling work covered the walls. The view from the balcony was a layered feast of flowered yards, downtown Boulder and the mountains overlooking the town.

One afternoon Robert and I walked to The Shambala Institute to attend a meditation class. As we sat, I became warmer and warmer until I was uncomfortably hot. The instructor said our energy shifts and intensifies during meditation, often causing a sensation of heat. We can feel high spiritual energy on mountains and near streams, waterfalls, and the sea, as well as in places where this energy cannot be attributed to nature.

At about 5 a.m. a few days later, I was wide awake, so I did some deep breathing, and asked for guidance. I went out-of-body, flying into a large room with television monitors showing the news on CNN about U.S. planes and a war, I think in Kosovo. Next I was on a long, wide path with red-brown dirt that stretched on and on, from the past to the future. As I walked past people lined up along the path, I knew they had been with me in previous lives. A young woman standing by the path kept looking at me; I walked over and we hugged each other. I continued walking, feeling energized and almost buoyant.

There were others I might have recognized farther along the path, but I couldn't see them clearly. I flew back to our room and noticed that the covers on my bed were pulled back. I was still in another dimension, and thought of going out again, but was tired and got back into bed, thinking about the many lives we all live.

A few days later I dreamed that everyone knew I was psychic and wanted me to give readings, which made me feel uncomfortable. I told one woman she had to find her own way. (I was telling myself that I have to find my own way). The dream also reflected the knowledge that I may not be able to help people in some circumstances. I'm reminded of Edgar Cayce's comment, when asked about having psychic readings— that it's all right, but the best source of information is our own knowing.

Another piece of advice came the next night, when I dreamed I was trying to organize my clothes and papers. A voice warned me to not write with insouciance (carelessness of feeling or an air of indifference). My dream was reminding me to think and write with care.

Later that year I had a surge of clients who told me of unusual occurrences in their lives. One of them talked about her precognition. As a young girl, it had frightened her, and she felt others would reject her if they knew she could 'see' what was going to happen in the future. She had shut it off then, but it had begun again. As an adult, she feels she can handle it now.

A policeman I was seeing for family problems told me there was something he had never told anyone, but…He had been driving his police car approaching an intersection, when two cars slid into each other. He said all of a sudden he was floating high over his seat, with his hands still on the wheel. It startled him and he slammed back down into the seat. He asked if he was crazy because he thought he was out of his body.

Another client told me about being able to 'read' others, to know what they were thinking. She used to believe everyone could do this, so she had closed herself off from others, hiding her private thoughts and feelings. She feared someone might use them against her, as in the past when she'd risked letting others get close to her. She feels more comfortable with her ability now, is not as guarded as she used to be and has begun to trust.

It can be difficult to accept extrasensory perception and to be open with others about it. As I struggle with the risk of sharing my innermost spiritual life, I meet more people who are in the same boat, looking for direction. It reinforces my determination to continue sharing. Besides picking up on other people's emotions, I began to adopt their physical feelings as well. I had suspected as much, but after one counseling session, I had no doubt.

A client, Sally, had the flu, but came in for her appointment anyway. Although she still wasn't feeling well, she thought she was no longer contagious. After a few minutes, a wave of weakness and nausea washed over me. I felt clammy, my nose was stopped up, and my throat and eyes began to itch. At first I thought I had caught the flu from her, but realized it would be impossible to catch it that quickly. I did not say anything, but as I listened to her talk, I began to breathe more deeply, telling myself to let the illness pass *through* me. Ten minutes later I was fine.

I had felt Sally's illness. I knew taking on her physical pain would not remove it, just as I had learned taking on another's emotional pain doesn't release theirs. Now, if I experience unexpected and unexplainable pain, I check to see if it's my own illness. If it's not, I let it go.

TWENTY TWO

*The greatest revolution of our generation is the discovery
that human beings, by changing the inner attitudes of
their minds, can change the outer aspects of their lives.*
William James

Several times I've been surprised by OBEs or dreams that
include spiritual helpers, sometimes with clues to clarify my life
purpose. One night I went out of body, and ended up at a
conference, waiting for the speaker. A tiny nun who looked like
Mother Teresa came up to me and asked if I remembered her. I
knew she was asking if I recalled her from a previous life. I said,
"No, but I wish I did." She was a caring teacher and spiritual
leader. She told me I was going to give birth and I said, "No, I'm
over 50." She replied that it did not matter. She meant I would
be giving birth to a new part of myself—a new phase of my life.

As I went to bed the night before a poetry conference I asked
my 'dream angel' for a dream with a limerick. I'd never written
one, and there was to be a contest. The next morning I woke
with a limerick running through my mind. At the conference,
I discovered this dream was connected to an out of body
experience I had four months earlier with the Venerable Bede.
I had known nothing about Bede, except that he was a religious
figure.

One of the poet-presenters had researched variations in
writing style at different times in history. I scanned the handout
he had prepared, and was startled to see a reference to Bede, and
that the earliest record of an English poem is Caedmon's Hymn
c.658 AD, written in Old English by Bede. Caedmon was a

sheep herder. When it was his turn around the campfire to recite or to sing a poem, he would run off and hide, because he did not know any. But in a dream one night, an angel gave him a poem. He recited it the next day, and it was a sensation, because it was a departure from the norm. It was a Praise poem rather than one about killing and maiming.

Since I had asked my dream angel for a limerick the night before, I thought that must be the connection between Bede and me, the reason he had been in one of my dreams months earlier. He was a monk, writer, poet and historian who wrote about the history of England and early Christianity who died in the eighth century.

I looked up my earlier dream and read about a child taking Venerable Bede at midnight in a blissful, white-light experience. I had the same experience, the light surrounding me as I moved higher and higher, until I felt myself connected with universal spirit that was pure bliss.

Another reference to Bede surfaced months later. While reading The Tibetan Book of Living and Dying, by Sogyal Rinpoche, I was surprised to come across this: "My favorite example (of a near-death experience) from history is the story told by the great English historian, the monk Bede, in the eighth century."

He describes Bede's tale of a man who came back from the dead and related that a guide had walked with him to a deep valley—out of the darkness into clear light. A wall reached out in all directions; then he was on top of the wall, looking out at a meadow filled with light. He was told by the guide to return to his body, and he did so reluctantly.

People who have near-death experiences describe a common pattern, though no two people have exactly the same experience. Bede, Sogyal Rinppcje, Raymond Moody and many others who have written about near-death experiences report some or all of the following:

1. Being in an altered state, with a sense of peace, without fear.
2. A buzzing or rushing sound, then separation from the body,

with the senses heightened, consciousness clear, seeing one's body, often from above, and the ability to move through walls.

3. Floating in space, and moving through a tunnel.
4. Being drawn toward a pinpoint of light, meeting a being of light, or being enveloped in light, and communicating with a 'presence' in a blissful and timeless dimension.
5. Seeing a world of beauty, hearing heavenly music and having a feeling of oneness.
6. Experiencing a life review.
7. Being pulled back to the physical or told to return.

Some have reported seeing a hellish place during an experience. It is much less common, but researcher P.M.H. Atwater describes a number of these in <u>Beyond the Light</u>. The core experience is the same for many out of body travelers, but without a life review.

My reminder of Bede at the poetry conference pushed aside a curtain to the spirit world that weekend, precipitating a visit from my mother. The next morning I woke up thinking of Mom and missing her, so I 'soul traveled' to another plane of existence where I found her. We shared stories until it was time for me to return, then we held each other tight. She showed me how we are connected now—as if our bones had melded together. Coming back to this dimension, I felt the clarity of that knowledge drift away from my awareness. While I am thankful for the information I receive from the other side, I often struggle to understand it or fit it into a pattern.

On another night, I heard the tinkle of chimes that sometimes signal a shift to another dimension. I flew out-of-body to Virginia Beach, to a beautiful house filled with light, with many windows and glass doors. It was close to the beach, and the circular drive in front was covered with crushed white shells or rocks. The living room had numerous candles, crystals, books, rocks and an aquarium. A kindly, older man walked in. He wore glasses and a cardigan sweater over a casual shirt and slacks. I thought he was the spirit of Edgar Cayce.

He said, "Welcome to the House of Everlasting Light." He told me he would be back, and left. On returning, he asked if I'd noticed a particular plaque; instructions were written on it about keeping a certain important rock underwater. Then he gave me a blessing, part of which was, "May a holy candle always keep you as bright as this." The feeling of peace, joy and light felt like a taste of the true spiritual beauty of the universe. I wondered about the significance of keeping the rock under water, but the whole experience felt like a continuation of my spiritual exploration. I felt a rush of positive feelings about the future.

TWENTY THREE

The unconscious has an extension that can reach anywhere, we have absolutely no means of establishing a definite frontier; as we cannot say where the world ends, so we cannot say where the unconscious ends, or whether it ends anywhere. C.G.Jung

Interested in learning more about energy healing, I attended a conference about it the following spring. It was sponsored by Harold McCoy (now deceased) of the Ozark Research Institute (ORI) in Arkansas. He, his wife Gladys, and other members of ORI do distance healing as well as hands-on healing, keeping records of the results of their work for research purposes. I had met Harold in Dallas and been impressed with his kindness, simplicity, and obvious gift for healing. He visualized the person he was working on, mentally 'unzipped' the top of his or her head and repaired damaged areas, using tools he visualized.

Energy healing involves letting go of our conscious will and asking Spirit to heal the person. Most healers preface their work with the intent that all help is only for the good. That week I watched participants, many of whom were medical doctors, nurses, or other health care professionals demonstrate their individual methods of healing. Though each of them had a slightly different approach, they all centered on positive, spiritual healing.

Sometime later, my husband benefited personally from the help of this spiritual group. Dean had been diagnosed by a heart specialist with an 80% to 90% blockage of his left carotid artery and partial blockage on the right side. His doctor ordered an angiogram to determine the exact location of the masses. Dean did not want to have surgery. I called ORI and asked that they use their distance healing skills on his behalf. We also focused on his receiving healing energy. By the time he went in for the test, he was feeling better, more alert.

After the test, the radiologist conducting the test came into the waiting room and told me Dean didn't need surgery. The blockage was at an acceptable level, about 50% on the left side. I said, "He's been working on that."

The doctor smiled. "Yes, that's what he told me." So much has been written about the benefits of prayer and energy healing, I wonder why we're still surprised.

Some aspects of my belief system were changing, but I continued to hold myself back. I wanted to let go my doubts on one level, but on another, I held onto them. I was not confident of my ability to channel healing energies, but I decided to try.

One night Dean was suffering with pain from arthritis; he went to bed early. By the time I got to bed he was asleep. I relaxed into a meditative state, asked for healing energy and almost immediately felt strong vibrations. I held my hands over Dean, and a few minutes later I was in the sky, in a spontaneous OBE. I heard a calm voice say, "You are never alone." I felt surrounded with love. The next morning Dean was much better.

I wish that whatever healing I can help effect occurred every time, but as those who do healing work have told me, "We can only ask that someone is healed. We aren't the healers, only the channel through which healing takes place." We can't always know what is best for a person. Sometimes the healing may take place inside, in the heart or spirit.

The next night I was out of body and began to feel anxious. In the past I would have stopped and returned to bed, but this time I stayed. I wanted to change old patterns and I received positive reinforcement for my risk. I felt as if every atom of my being became enlivened and energized, and I had a sense of perfect well-being. I watched a meteor shower in awe. The stars were beautiful as they streaked across the heavens. I was rewarded with the mystical experience of joining with the white light, a blissful sensation of oneness and of total peace and love.

It brought an absolute understanding of the universe, of past, present and future, with the certainty that all is as it should be. Memory faded on my return, but the experience left a residue of faith and love, and the knowledge I would someday return. My experiences and dreams led me to the belief that my life purpose is to focus on my own spiritual growth and encourage others to focus on theirs.

One of my clients, Darla, had a painful back problem and feared she needed surgery, which she dreaded. She had a strong faith in God, and I asked her if she had asked her friends to pray for her. She had not. She said she had already had her share of miracles. Years earlier she had experienced intense stomach pain, and x-rays showed a growth in her abdomen. The doctors said her only option was surgery. Many people prayed for her before and during her operation. Her doctors were shocked when they could find no sign of the growth. They replaced 'all her parts,' sewed her back up, and told her they couldn't explain how the growth had disappeared. She knew the answer, and unofficially at least, the doctors concurred. Prayer had done the work.

When she told me this, I asked if she thought God was limited, doling out miracles one to a person. She said, "No," and laughed. She went home and called her friends to ask for their prayers. The next time I saw her, she said the doctors suggested an interim procedure that would delay the surgery. So far she hasn't had to undergo the operation she dreads, but if she does in the future, faith and prayers will accompany her.

Further validation of the reality of healing experiences like Darla's, and those in my own dreams and OBEs occurred at one of my high school reunions.

I had been looking forward to talking with one of my former classmates. Mary had been present in one of my past life experiences—one in which disciples of Jesus were waiting to hear whether he was dead. Mary and I had recognized each other, but had not spoken. I was curious to see if she'd had a dream or similar experience. When I looked through my journals, I was reminded that she had been in several of my OBEs and lucid dreams.

I especially wanted to ask her about an OBE that took place about six months earlier. I wanted to explore my childhood home, and flew north, ending not far from my parent's home in Belleville. I saw Mary, and asked her if she knew she'd been in some of my dreams. She said she did. Then she told me she had cancer in a female part of her body. I told her about spiritual healing and said I thought I could help her. When she agreed, I held my hand over her to bring in healing energy and told her not to worry, that she would be fine. She was satisfied, and we parted. Since I was out of body, I didn't expect her to remember this, or be consciously aware of it, but thought she might have perceived it as a dream.

At the reunion, 35 or 40 women were crammed into a tiny noisy room, catching up with friends from long ago. Toward the end of the evening, Mary and I were at the same table. A friend, Joan, asked me if I was writing another poetry book.

"Not right now," I said. "I'm working on a book about mystical and spiritual events, including intuition, spirit and angel experiences, synchronicity and dreams."

Joan said, "I know about that. We noticed a lot of coincidences during Bob's last weeks." Her husband had died three years earlier.

After one or two other women shared their stories about synchronicities I brought up the topic of dreams. I told Mary she had been in several of mine.

"Why would you dream about me?" she asked.

"I don't know. Have I been in any of your dreams?"

"I don't remember dreams. What did you dream about me?"

"I'll tell you. But first, do you believe in life after death and in reincarnation?"

"I believe we continue in spirit after our death. I'm not sure what to think about reincarnation."

I told her about my past-life experience (I called it a dream, assuming OBEs were too strange for this Catholic group of friends) during the time of Christ's death and resurrection. "Everyone was waiting to hear if Jesus was dead. You were there, and I could tell you recognized me too, but we didn't speak. I was sad, because I knew Jesus *had* died then when I thought about it later, I remembered Jesus had risen. "Maybe it was a lesson that what seems to be an end can sometimes be a beginning," I said.

"Maybe," Mary said. "But I wonder why I was there."

I said, "So do I. Another dream happened on my mom's birthday, March 10. You were sick, and we talked about healing with spiritual energy. I put my hand on you and asked for healing then I told you that you would be fine."

Mary's eyes widened. "I had surgery for breast cancer on March 10 and began radiation therapy on March 20. And I *am* well now. That dream was true."

I didn't tell Mary that in my 'dream' her illness was cancer of 'a female part of her body,' because I did not want to cause distress if she had not already had cancer. Healing can be many things, and sometimes not what the individual needs for their own spiritual fulfillment. I learned from the dowsers to ask for what is for the best for the person and for the greatest good.

There was another classmate, Jane, with whom I had considered discussing an OBE in which she was ill and I helped her. For some reason I was hesitant to talk to her about it, maybe because I was afraid she would scoff. Incidents from almost a half-century earlier had evidently had left residual scarring on my ego. I bumped up against my fear of exposure. Being different could bring teasing and criticism. I thought of my past-life memory of being 'thrown to the lions,' and my discovery that although it can be frightening to risk exposure, we are never alone. Dreams didn't seem as odd as OBEs. Again, I decided to label it a dream if I talked to her about it.

At the reunion I was surprised to see her using a cane. I heard she had a stroke a couple of years earlier. On the last night of the reunion, she told me she was disappointed that we had not had a chance to visit. I asked her to join me for breakfast the next day and she said she would love to. I was curious about whether or not Jane had experienced energy healing or if she had a dream about this.

That morning, as we lingered over coffee, I told her about the experience (again labeling it a dream)—that I was sitting with her on a large, square, cement floor, the foundation of a building without ceiling or walls. She was very thin, and I thought she was dying from cancer. A tube ran from the back of her head under the skin and down her neck and back. I held her, my hands drawing healing energy from the universe to ease her pain, and it helped.

I told her she was braver than I would have expected. I also said I tried to be inconspicuous, and it crossed my mind that I might be more effective if I were not trying to be unnoticed. I didn't know if I could heal her, but hoped I could ease her pain. She became more energized and said her pain had lessened. I was amazed at how much better she was.

I said, "It doesn't seem like a stroke would affect you that way.

Jane said, "That was the cancer, a year after my stroke. The tube coming from my head was from the surgery. They removed a huge melanoma from my lower back and there were tubes everywhere."

Later, when we got back upstairs, she showed me the saucer-shaped indentation in her lower back. We may believe in the benefits of prayer, but when we experience those benefits ourselves, our belief solidifies.

TWENTY FOUR

Before enlightenment chopping wood,
carrying water. After enlightenment,
chopping wood, carrying water.

Zen Proverb

It can be hard to act on a new belief. Neither Marguerite nor I were surprised at the positive results we saw when others dowsed, but we weren't sure of our own abilities. It can help to have a friend give you a little push.

A few weeks after my reunion, Marguerite and I spent a day together, catching up. She had been at her brother's farm in Oklahoma, helping him clean the house and getting his belongings into a semblance of order. She said the house was spilling over with the accumulation of years and it was hard to find things. Her brother had placed a large sum of money in an envelope and put it somewhere for safekeeping, then forgotten where that safe place was. They had torn the house apart looking for it, without success.

Marguerite asked me if I would try dowsing for it. When I agreed, she drew an outline of the house and gave me her pendulum to use. Besides misplacing the money, her brother's wallet had recently disappeared. He thought it might have fallen from his pocket when he was operating a tractor in one of his fields. "Maybe you can dowse for that too," Marguerite said. "The envelope with the money is the most important thing, but he would still like to find the wallet."

I had never seriously tried to locate lost items using dowsing, but I agreed. We had nothing to lose. She drew a primitive diagram outlining the rooms in the house, the garage, driveway, barns and the surrounding fields.

I held the pendulum by the tiny smooth stone at one end of the slender chain. A slightly larger, polished stone was attached to the other end. I twirled it in a circle to determine which way the pendulum would move to signal a 'yes.' It moved back and forth. Then I did the same thing for 'no,' and the pendulums moved from side to side. If I got a 'yes' response to a particular location, Marguerite would check it out the next time she visited her brother.

I moved the pendulum over her drawings, asking Spirit for help finding the lost money. Nothing happened for long minutes and I was beginning to wonder if anything would. But when I moved it over the outline of the den, the pendulum began swinging back and forth in a vigorous yes. There was another positive response on one side of the laundry room. Marguerite said they had already torn the den apart, finding nothing, and that the laundry room was nearly empty. She did not think the money or wallet could be in either place, but when I tried again, I got a "yes" response at the same two places.

Marguerite said, "I'll look in the den again, but I don't hold out much hope. There are bookcases on that wall, and we've already taken all the books off the shelves. We shook out each one. We looked in every possible nook and cranny in that room *and* in the laundry room."

A week later she phoned. "Are you sitting down?"

"Yes," I said, pulling up a chair.

She said she had gone to the farm over the weekend and had torn the den apart again, telling her brother that her dowser friend said the money might be there. No luck. She spotted a slim plastic folder she hadn't noticed before, between the sofa and the bookcase. She thought she had found the money, but when she unzipped the folder, it was empty. Then she noticed a second, smaller zipper on the side and opened it. The money was there! She and her brother were ecstatic.

The next day as she was leaving for home, her brother, no longer a skeptic, asked her to have me dowse for his wallet.

When Marguerite found the money in the folder, she had been so excited she forgot about the missing wallet. I reminded her I had already had a positive response around one wall of the mud room. She was so sure it couldn't be there, I agreed to dowse again the next time I was at her house.

She still had the paper and pencil drawing she'd made, and once again I held the pendulum over it, concentrating on the missing wallet. The only positive response came when I held it over a laundry room wall—the same wall as before. Marguerite was disappointed, but agreed to look one more time. A week later she called to tell me they had found the wallet. It was where the pendulum had indicated, but on the other side of the wall, in a bathroom closet. It had not occurred to her to look there before, but when she opened the closet door to get something, the wallet was sitting right in front of her. Locating both the missing money and the wallet solidified my belief that we can connect with Spirit to find answers.

Despite the dowsing success and the validation of some of my out-of-body and precognitive dreams, I still felt cautious about sharing my experiences with others. Apprehension about being disbelieved or ridiculed held me back. I'd begun writing this book, but had not decided if I would seek publication. I admired those who shared their own stories, aware that it may have been hard for them to write about own personal thoughts, feelings and experiences.

Sophy Burnham, author of several angel books, has written that she was apprehensive about writing The Ecstatic Journey, a more personal story. Raymond Moody speaks and writes freely about life after death and his work on communication with spirits, but admits it is harder to relate his own story.

It was a struggle to decide how open I wanted to be when speaking and writing about my mystical and paranormal experiences, but when the workshop organizer for a spiritual retreat called and asked me if I would be a presenter I said yes. I decided to lead two workshops—one about OBEs in general, the other on how to use soul travels to help others.

The speakers that weekend stimulated a sense of spiritual

connection, often using guided imagery to help us relax and find answers to our own questions. One of my favorite visualizations is to picture myself walking through serene woods, then into a building, down a hallway and into Carl Jung's study, where Jung sits at his desk, reading. Books in the room have answers to many questions. Jung says when he is confused or looking for information, he comes into that room. He points toward a door and says he sometimes walks through it to find answers. The visualization helps us find answers that are within, which we have not been able to access.

When it was time for me to give my workshop, I was excited about helping facilitate soul travel for those who attended, and was surprised and pleased to find the room full. Some had already experienced NDEs or OBEs and shared their stories, describing thoughts and feelings, and expressing their interest in further exploration. Others who had not yet experienced that change in consciousness talked about why they wanted to try. Some of them had hovered on the edge, letting their fears stop them, as I had in the past.

Our small room that day was far from ideal, with a very rough, uneven stone floor. It was impossible to lie down on the quilts and blankets we'd brought, so we sat on straight-back chairs from the dining room and lawn chairs from the terrace. I turned on a tape of relaxing wind chimes and music, and we began. Despite their discomfort, everyone quickly drifted off into a relaxed state. One of the women, sitting on a very straight chair, nodded into what seemed a deep sleep, and her head bobbed around so wildly I was afraid she would fall. I pulled my chair closer to her so I could catch her if she toppled over.

After about twenty minutes I brought them back to aware-ness, and they began to talk about what had happened. One woman said she'd had a near-death experience years earlier and it had been so incredible that until now she hadn't wanted to attempt to leave her body again. She said, "I was afraid it would be a letdown, like a 'Walmart thing.' Don't get me wrong, I love to shop, but ..." She paused then began again. "Today I left my body ... as soon as we started. I flew around in the clouds, circled down toward the ground and found myself right over the Walmart in our neighborhood. It was fun, though. I guess I don't have to wait till I die again to take a few little trips."

As we went around the circle sharing, most people were pleased with the results of their efforts. Only one woman said nothing had happened; she was curious, but was afraid to leave her body and stopped herself from doing so. Everyone was eager for the follow-up workshop the next day.

For the second workshop I planned to talk about using OBEs for positive purposes, like receiving lessons, healing others and leading lost souls into the light. I had never spoken on this topic before, nor had I tried to teach others how to develop this ability.

There were even more people at this session. It was held in a larger, more private and comfortable room, on the second floor of a lodge. The room was carpeted, furnished with a few tables and chairs, but most of the men and women chose to relax on blankets and pillows on the floor. Since some of the participants were new, I briefly went over the information from the day before, taking time to answer a few questions. After talking about the positive intentions they might express before their soul travels, I started the relaxing sounds of a tape and began a gentle guidance into whatever dimensions they chose to explore. I could see everyone from where I sat, and could tell, by the shifts in their breathing patterns, that most of them had relaxed and let go of their conscious tensions fairly soon.

One man, Paul, told us the day before that he traveled out-of-body easily and often. After a few minutes he moved his arms, holding them slightly off the floor in an open position, as if in offering or prayer. Then he pulled them in toward his body in a protective position and the expression on his face changed from unlined serenity to a slight frown. His face had seemed light at first, as if lit from within, but as he drew his arms in close, his face darkened. A little later, he relaxed and moved his arms to the floor at his side. His face smoothed and his breathing slowed.

Soon after, I asked everyone to begin stretching, to come back into awareness of the room. Paul stood and walked toward the screen door. He seemed agitated, and I asked if he was all right. He assured me he was, but thought he needed to "get myself together" before he shared with the group, that he didn't want to upset anyone. After a few minutes on the balcony, he came back inside and related his experience to us.

He said he'd left his body as soon as we began, and flew over Paris, then remembered why he had left his body—to try to help lost spirits move on. He found himself at a graveyard for soldiers who died during the Civil War. He was met with waves of grief, despair and anger, and heard voices pleading for help and cursing with rage. He did not see them, but heard and felt many spirits trapped in their pain. He said he had never had such an overwhelming experience. After a short time he told them that he had to leave, but would return to help.

"As soon as I was back in this room, I understood what had happened. I was overcome with emotion, partly because in a past life I was a soldier during that time. I know I can handle those emotions next time. I am going back to help those lost souls." The raw, negative fear, anger and grief had shocked him, and he had let the spirits' grief become his own.

A number of people in the group were healers, and Paul's experience led to a discussion about how we can take care of ourselves when doing spiritual work. Several participants reported less dramatic OBEs, and a few said they let their anxiety stop them, but thought they were closer to 'letting go' than they'd been in the past. They might be able to do so in a more private setting. Many felt vibrations, heard a loud sound that often signals an OBE, or felt a separation in which they were just above or next to the body. Several were relieved to learn that the physical sensations that frightened them are normal when leaving the body. They had the same fears I did twenty-five years earlier, and a few others. I assured them they would have no trouble getting back into their bodies if they left them.

A young woman said she had fought the sensation of being pulled out of her body for a long time, because she feared her family would think she was crazy or evil. Another woman had been fighting spontaneous OBEs because she was afraid of the unknown. Hearing how others felt safe going out of body helped her release her fears.

That night in our bunk beds, we talked about the events of the day. Susie had missed my workshop. She said she would like to try to go out of body. She didn't fear it the way she used to, but she didn't think she could. I told her she only needed to have the intention, relax and let go. We were both tired and I fell into a restless sleep right away, tossing and turning. I was half-awake when I heard a bed creak and someone walk across the room. Then I felt someone pat me on the back. I fell into sleep again.

The next morning Susie told me I had been restless after going to bed. She had thought of telling me I was OK, and patting me on the back, but I began to sleep quietly. She said she had been outside the cabin, out-of-body, but as soon as she realized she'd left her body she was pulled back in.

"I wish I could have stayed out longer. And that I could have helped you," she said.

"You did. I heard you climb out of the top bunk, walk across the room, and felt you pat me on the back. Your spirit left your body to comfort me before you went outside. Most people do get anxious at first, but next time you're aware you're 'out,' remind yourself you are safe."

The retreat had been a success. We talked about it at our next dream group meeting, and Frances told me she had incubated a dream for me. The last couple of meetings we had taken turns being the recipient of a dream by each of us. At bedtime we would remind ourselves of our intent to have a dream for that person. Frances hadn't been able to dream for me when it was my turn. She said she worked on it while I was gone and the results were interesting. In her dream I was a nurse and a teacher, showing children how to 'travel.' The dream validated my decision to share out-of-body experiences in healing and in helping spirits move to the light.

For the last few years, during dreams and altered states of consciousness I've been told to record what happened. Guides, angels and spirits, including my mother and father, have offered guidance. I have finally learned to recognize and appreciate mystical gifts, synchronicities and lessons. I've made that leap of faith I didn't understand as a child.

The very word mystical is defined as a spiritual meaning or reality that is neither apparent to the senses nor obvious to the intelligence. It involves, or has the nature of, direct, subjective communication with God.

Mysticism is the belief that direct knowledge of God, spiritual truth or ultimate reality can be attained through subjective experience, intuition or insight. It is the direct experience of God, of spiritual encounters transcending human comprehension that lead to joy and heightened or expanded energy, increased compassion for others and a deepening capacity to love.

A mystic is one who seeks by contemplation and self-surrender to obtain union with, or absorption into the Deity, or who believes in the spiritual apprehension of truths inaccessible to understanding.

I used to think such people were only saints from the far distant past. They are more common than I could ever have imagined. Many of us are so busy with our day to day lives we leave little time or thought to the eternal lives of our souls. Yet we are good people. We try not to hurt others, to bring goodness into the world, to love and care for others. None of that is wrong. But there is more.

TWENTY FIVE

All man's miseries derive from not being able
to sit quietly in a room alone.   Blaise Pascal

Blessed with all the loving people in my life, as well as the continuing lessons I received, I hoped I was on the right path. One night at bedtime, I meditated and asked, as I had before, if there was anything further I could do to clarify my life purpose. A voice replied, "It's not time yet. No need."

I offered to help in some way, felt rapid vibrations, and was instantly out of body and flying through the sky. I found myself alone in a classroom at a small boarding school in France was during War II. I was Mother Superior of a small community of nuns and principal of the school. The long, heavy habit and confining head-piece of the order felt natural to me. As I looked around the room I became anxious. I was not afraid for myself, but for the children. I realized soldiers would be storming in soon, looking for Jewish children they suspected we were hiding. They were always suspicious of us, but this time they were not wrong.

I rushed over to my desk and pulled incriminating papers from the bottom of my workbox. They must be hidden, for they could mean a death sentence to the children. I knelt on the dark, wax-smoothed floor, my heavy silver cross and wooden rosary beads clanking against a rough box I pulled from a space beneath wide oak planks. I put the papers in the box, then said, "No, not safe enough." I removed the papers, put the box back, pushed the board in place and quickly walked across the room to a door that led to the basement stairs.

In the dim light, I scanned the box-laden shelves that lined the walls on either side of the stairs as I walked down, but hiding the papers there didn't feel safe either. I crossed to the furnace, tearing the pages into tiny pieces before feeding them to the fire. I watched as the flames consumed the documents. Preserving the information on those pages could not be as important as the lives of five children.

It was imperative that I return to the classroom before the soldiers arrived, to avoid arousing their suspicions further. Near the top of the stairs I stopped, took off my white cotton gloves, now gray with soot, and dropped them to the floor below. They would probably not be seen there, and if they were, would not mean anything to the soldiers. Smoothing my heavy woolen skirts, I took a deep breath and pushed open the door. The classroom was still empty. My job was finished.

Instantly I was back in my bed in Dallas, gratified that I had been able to help save the children. It had seemed perfectly natural to be in that classroom, wearing nun's clothing and identity, but it did not seem like a past life. Since I was born into this life in 1936, I could not have been a nun in France during World War II. But I knew I had been.

Space and time are not the same when we leave this dimension. We may lead dual lives. Another possibility is that we (souls) can shift to other dimensions of both time and space to give assistance to others in the past. How relative is time? I had never thought about the ability we have to impact the past. If something has already happened, can we be instrumental in making changes in the past; if so, how? The universe exists on many dimensions. If it is possible for us to be instrumental in affecting the past, it isn't impossible to imagine that others (in future dimensions) could influence our lives.

Another recent experience that fits the concept of past, present and future interactions reinforces the possibility of how we can help others after we shift to higher levels of consciousness.

During an OBE I was suddenly standing in a dark, empty room in nineteenth century Ireland, during the potato famine.

A man walked down the stairs. He brought a sad, heavy feeling into the room with him. He had drenched the shoulder of what must have been his one good jacket with oil or gasoline. His wife and seven or eight children trailed down the stairs into the room. The man was fearful of the future and had lost all hope. I was sure he planned to kill himself and his family. I told the woman and children to run next door. They looked confused, but did as I told them.

I touched the man's arm and said, "Don't do it. I've come from the future to help." It surprised me to hear the words come out of my mouth, but I knew it was true.

He said, "The children are gone now. I can't hurt them," as if his own life was worth nothing. He still meant to kill himself.

"Please don't," I said. "Your children need you alive! They love you. If you do this it will hurt them for the rest of their lives. I came from the future to help you. I can't stay, but others are also coming to help."

He sobbed with relief as I held him.

"They will come," I said. "I promise." I knew he would be all right, and in an instant I was back in my hotel room. A sheet billowed up to the ceiling, as if from a puff of wind. I clutched it and pulled it down over me, aware it was the curtain that delineates dimensions.

Not long after my 'visit' to Ireland, I experienced a lucid dream in which my family was to meet with the Dalai Lama, Supreme Tibetan leader, and other priests and holy men and women, including the seventeenth Karmapa, head of the Karma Kagyer sect of Tibetan Buddhism. This teenage monk fled China in January, 2000 and was granted refugee status in India, where he reclaimed the traditional black crown that had been kept in the Rumtek Monastery for 18 years.

In the dream: *We were to meet with them in Arizona. I suggested to my family that we not arrive until the second day, to give the priests time to talk and pray together. When we joined them, the Karmapa had just finished telling about his difficult journey. The Dalai Lama laughed, saying, "Isn't it wonderful?" He sees joy in everything.*

143

It reminded me of the time my daughter had been feeling discouraged and heard Mom's voice say, "Isn't this an adventure?" When I become impatient for answers or wonder where the next part of my path will lead, I remind myself that it is truly the journey that is important. We will all reach our destination, but the questions are when and how? When we find answers, they always seem to lead to more questions. Life is an adventure.

The night after my dream about the lamas, I had a dream that triggered memory of one I'd had a year earlier. On the first occasion, I had wakened my husband to tell him I'd had an important dream. I asked him to remember it for me because I was too sleepy to write it on my notepad. As ridiculous as that request sounds, he said he would. I tried to think of a sentence to condense the dream that would trigger exact recall the next day. I came up with, "I am twelve years old, and the decisions I make about events that occur today will affect the rest of my life."

Dean did remember, and repeated the exact words to me the next day, but I had no memory of the dream. I was disappointed. I had been careless, and the dream escaped me completely. I hoped I would have the dream again, and a year later when I did, I made sure to write all of it I could recall.

I'm twelve years old, at home with Mom, Dad, Jim and John. I'm sitting on the back porch steps, enjoying the wonderful fresh air. It's beginning to get dark and lights are on inside the house. It is nearly dinnertime, but I want to stay out a little longer. There is a flicker of light in the sky. I hear a swelling of music. An angel glides down, says something... I can't recall all of it, but I do remember... "the decisions you make about the events that occur that day will affect the rest of your life." I ask, "Will the book be published?" and hear, "Yes." There is a feeling of light shifting and the powerful sound in the air softens, stops. I see several angels, and hear them talking. One says, "You had better go inside now." I do, and everyone has already eaten, but Mom fixes a plate for me.

I think the dream is identical to the one I had asked Dean to remember. I probably had a mystical experience at age twelve, or maybe even earlier. I do know I am being helped, guided and protected, as are we all. My question about publishing my book seems odd now, but in the dream it didn't. Even at twelve I knew I wanted to write.

As I mentioned earlier, sometimes I need a firm and obvious shove before I pay attention to intuition or dream messages. Wherever my path leads, I have learned the journey *is* the adventure, and teaching, healing, writing and helping others toward the light are part of it. Many of the questions I've asked myself have been answered, but every answer, every experience, raises new questions.

Most of my doubts about spiritual, mystical events have dissolved. I've come to accept that the mystical experience is ineffable, not capable of being entirely put into words, though there are still times I'm impatient with the mystery of it all. My road, like many, is an up and down journey.

I began writing with the hope I could help others by sharing my experiences and encouraging them to share theirs, to "come out of the spiritual closet." I have been fortunate to meet spiritual teachers, healers, and others with gifts of psychic ability, who generously share their wisdom and skills with others. They all emphasize the importance of prayer and meditation as a means of spiritual awakening and growth, a search for the God within. Religions are man-made and are about beliefs, while spiritual has to do with actual experience.

In order to learn and grow spiritually, I want to be open to the possibilities that offer themselves. We are living on this earth to find and appreciate the joys that life and its relationships offer as well. Finding balance between the spiritual and physical world isn't always easy, and the balance is shifting. Predictions for the new millennium do include physical earth changes, but the more significant changes are spiritual. We are moving toward a universal memory, awareness of ourselves as spiritual beings, residing in temporary material bodies. We each have our own paths to follow, but as we connect more and more with Spirit, we understand that all paths lead to the same place.

By paying attention to our intuitive voices, and noticing and appreciating the meaningful coincidences in our lives, we can release our fear of the unknown. The acceptance of NDEs as a valid reality has opened the door to knowing the dimension of spirit is always available to us. We can connect with this level of consciousness and learn—through dreams, OBEs and psychic and intuitive knowing, as well as through prayer, song, chant and meditation. Angels, guides and spirits surround us, helping and inspiring us, ready for us to open our hearts and ask for guidance. We are on the journey together.

APPENDIX I

OUT-OF-BODY-EXPERIENCES (OBEs)

Always begin with the pure intention of benefiting all beings. Whether you have already experienced one or more OBEs or not, the following tips will be useful.

CAVEATS

Once you have opened the door to other dimensions, you will almost certainly become more sensitive to other paranormal events, such as clairvoyance, intuition and synchronicity.

Second, if the idea of trusting your inner self, while letting go of your cognitive earth self is difficult for you to imagine, it will be hard to effect an OBE. An important step is letting go.

Third, you may experience anxiety, a general fear of the unknown, before or during an OBE, but once you are out, fear evaporates. Don't worry about getting back into your body. It happens easily, without conscious effort. Just 'think' yourself back in body, and you're there.

Fourth, you may sometimes have the sensation of sleep paralysis. In this condition, your mind is awake before your body fully wakens. It can be frightening, because it is impossible to move for a brief time. Wait a minute and your body will catch up with your mind; then you will have no difficulty moving. The practice of visualizing yourself surrounded by white light can help you feel safe.

GETTING READY

Meditation, hypnosis, dreams, lucid dreams, deep relaxation, mystical events and OBEs occur when you are in an altered state of consciousness. If you meditate or practice deep relaxation, you have a head start. If not, it may take a little more time to prepare.

To begin, find a quiet place where you won't be interrupted.

Lie down and close your eyes. Be sure that your body is in a comfortable position. Lying on your back, feet uncrossed, is optimum for most of us. Start to breathe more deeply as you think about what you want to do; 'let go' and leave your body. If you are too drowsy or too tired, you might fall asleep, so it is better to try this when you're not feeling exhausted.

THE EXPERIENCE

Give yourself suggestions such as, "I'm going to let go and have an out-of-body-experience," or "My body is relaxing, I am safe, and I am leaving my body now." Repeat your own suggestions several times as you relax. Then tell yourself that with every breath, your body becomes more and more relaxed. Imagine yourself floating up from your body peacefully.

Focus on the stillness and the dark. Imagine a spot several inches in front of your eyes and visualize yourself moving toward the spot, lifting up then flying toward the stars. Let yourself imagine the feeling of flying as you breathe slowly and deeply, becoming more relaxed, yet staying mentally alert.

Begin to breathe in quick, short breaths with your mouth slightly open. Notice any physical sensations in your body. You may have a sense of lightness, or feel vibrations.

Although not everyone feels them, many people who have had multiple OBEs report feeling vibrations, ranging from a slight tremor to large, almost bed-bouncing motion. If you do feel vibrations, focus on them, allowing them to increase. Do not try to stop them or imagine them away. You might notice you can feel movement inside your body—your heartbeat, movement in your abdomen or the sense of blood moving through your veins. Anything that pulls your attention to the internal physical body, while shutting away outside thoughts, will help you achieve your goal.

At about the same time, you might hear or feel a buzzing sound or noise from inside your head. Focus on the sound, allowing it to increase. You are about to go out-of-body.

There are a number of ways to initiate an OBE, and after

you've experienced it several times and have more confidence in yourself, you may find it easy and fun to try other techniques. Like anything else, the more you practice, the easier it becomes. Try various relaxation methods to find what works best for you. If it's difficult to shift into a relaxed state of being, playing relaxation tapes may help.

You'll find the ability to relax and 'let go' comes in handy for things besides OBEs. For instance, if you are going to spend time in the dentist's chair, you might as well enjoy it. When you go in, practice relaxation. Visualize colors, especially green and pink, which are soothing and healing colors. You might find you have to work to stay awake. It is not possible to be relaxed and anxious at the same time.

GOING OUT-OF-BODY FROM A DREAM

Some people find it easier to begin an OBE while dreaming. If you'd like to try this, tell yourself at bedtime that you're going to notice you're dreaming, and that when something unusual or out of the ordinary occurs in a dream, you'll ask yourself if it is a dream. When you ask, you'll become aware that you *are* dreaming, and you can direct or change what is happening. You can fly out of body, return then leave again if you want. You are probably already going out-of-body from dreams but are unaware of it. Be sure to remind yourself before drifting off to sleep that you're going to not only *notice* you are dreaming, but will remember the experience.

WHEN OUT-OF-BODY, TRY THESE

1. Look at your body resting in bed as you float above it.
2. Look at yourself in a mirror.
3. Walk or leap through walls, windows, doors, ceilings.
4. If you're afraid, poke your hand through first then follow.
5. Fly. It's natural and easy when out-of-body.
6. Think of where you want to go—and go there.
7. Look at your hands and feet. Are they transparent?

8. Pay attention to your five earth senses. Ask for clarity.
9. Notice the sensation of flight—the air on your body.
10. When you meet others, you can communicate with thought.
11. Write down everything you can remember.
12. While you're 'out,' ask for information.

WHERE DO YOU GO?

Once you've let yourself out where can you go? What can you do? Remember that while you're out of body *you are spirit*, connected to universal consciousness without the encumbrance of your earth-plane life and body. For some, just exploring in and around the house is enough at first, while for others, flying into the sky and visiting other dimensions and universes is the goal. Or you might ask to have a past life experience.

This is one time that travel is free, fast, and you can return any time you wish. You might find you return unexpectedly if you lose focus or if a noise or uncomfortable body sensation pulls you back.

ASKING FOR HELP

It can be wonderful to have a guide or angel with you, and there is no reason you shouldn't ask for one when you get ready to explore. Have your intention in mind (going out-of-body) and ask a guide or angel to help you—to go with you. Then begin your deep breathing, focus, and let go.

Keep a journal about your OBEs. Write as soon as possible, then go back to sleep. You can look at what you've written the next day, and elaborate on it, filling in the blanks so you are clear, or you'll lose a good part of the experience and not be able to access the memory later.

HELPING OTHERS

After you're comfortable with OBEs you can ask your angels or guides what you can do to help others. Whether you see them or not, they are with you. You might visit the past or future to find where you can be of service. Or you might learn to use your vibrational energy to send healing to a relative, a friend, or even to someone you have never met. Always ask for the greatest good when you do this.

You could find yourself directing departed souls (who are 'stuck') toward the light. When you find yourself in any of those circumstances, you will know what to do. And you'll be safe. You are the inner self, or spirit, and your earth-body self is safe at home in bed, waiting for spirit self to return. There is nothing to fear. If you need extra reassurance, talk to your angel, and remember to visualize yourself in the white light.

You might experience a mystical oneness with the universe in a blissful, golden white light. Your out of body experiences will be as unique to you as your three-dimensional earth experiences are. By telling yourself to pay attention, to notice, and to remember, you'll increase your awareness and memory of dream states as well as your OBEs. Do not discount small shifts in dimension. People have told me they felt as if they were floating just above their bodies, but decided that couldn't be true, so ignored it and went to sleep. Don't ignore those feelings. Build on them. Decide you want to go higher or farther, breathe deeply and let go. Just think of what you want, let go your thoughts, and trust. *Remember, it is the journey that is important.*

Appendix II   ORGANIZATIONS

ASSOCIATION FOR RESEARCH AND ENLIGHTENMENT
215 67th Street
Virginia Beach, VA 23451-2061

INSTITUTE OF NOETIC SCIENCES
475 Gate Five Road, Suite 300
Sausalito, CA 94965-0909

OZARK RESEARCH INSTITUTE, INC.
P.O. Box 387   Fayetteville, AR 72702-0387
http://www.ozarkresearch.org

APPENDIX III   SUGGESTED READINGS

Abbott, Edwin. Flatland. Dover Pub. Inc. N.Y. 1992.

Andrews, Ted. Animal-Speak. Llewellyn Pub., MN. 1998.

Atwater, P.M.H. Coming Back to Life. Citadel Press. N.Y. 2001.

------ Near-Death Experiences. MJF Books. N.Y. 2011.

Borysenko, Joan. Fire in the Soul. Warner Books. N.Y. 1993.

------The Ways of the Mystic. Hay House Inc., CA. 1997.

Brinkley, Dannion. Saved By the Light. Villard Books, N.Y. 1994.

------ At Peace in the Light. Harper Paperbacks, N.Y. 1995.

Burnham, S. The Ecstatic Journey. Ballentine Books. N.Y. 1997.

Castenada, Carlos. The Teaching of Don Juan. Washington Square Press. N.Y. 1968.

Cayce, Hugh L. Venture Inward. A.R.E. Press, VA, 1964.

Cerminara, Gina. Many Lives Many Loves. DeVorss & Co.Pub. 1963.

Chopra, Deepak. The Way of the Wizard. Harmony Books, N.Y. 1995.

Dalai Lama. The Four Noble Truths. Thorsons.London. 1997.

Dossey, Larry. M.D. Healing Words. Harper. San Fran. 1993.

------ Space, Time & Medicine. Shambhala. Boston. 1993.

Eben, Alexander, M.D. The Map of Heaven, Simon & Schuster. N.Y. 2014.

Elliot, William. Tying Rocks to Clouds. Quest Books. IL. 1995.

Evans-Wentz, W.Y., ed. The Tibetan Book of the Dead. Oxford U. Press, London. 1960.

Garrett, Eileen J. My Life As a Search for the Meaning of Mediumship. Rider & Co. London. 1939.

Grant, Robert J. Are We Listening To the Angels? A.R.E. Press, VA, 1994.

------Universe of Worlds. A.R.E. Press. VA. 2003.

Guiley, Rosemary. The Encyclopedia of Dreams. Berkley Books. N.Y. 1995.

Hartzell, Harmon, Bro, Ph.C. Edgar Cayce On Religion and Psychic Experience. Coronet Com. N.Y. 1970.

Holzer, Hans. Life Beyond Life. Parker Pub. Co. N.Y. 1985.

Kirkpatrick, Sidney. Edgar Cayce, An American Prophet. Riverhead Books. Penguin Putnam, Inc. NY. 2000.

MacLaine, Shirley. Going Within. Bantam Books. N.Y. 1989.

Mitchell, Dr.Edgar. The Way of the Explorer. G.P.Putnam's Sons. N.Y. 1996.

Moen, Bruce. Voyages into the Unknown. Hampton Roads Pub.Co.1997.

Monroe, Robert. Journeys Out Of the Body. Doubleday. N.Y. 1971.

Montgomery, Ruth. A World Beyond. Fawcett Pub. Conn. 1971.

Moody, Raymond, M.D. Life After Life. Bantam Books, N.Y. 1975.

Moody, Raymond, M.D. and Perry, Paul. Reunions Villard Books, N.Y., 1993.

Morse, Melvin, M.D., and Perry, Paul. Closer To the Light, Ivy Books. N.Y. 1990.

Mother Teresa. In My Own Words. Gramercy Books. 1996.

Myss, Caroline. Anatomy of the Spirit. Harmony Books. N.Y. 1996.

Orloff, Judith, M.D. Second Sight. Warner Books, N.Y. 1996.

Reed, Henry. Edgar Cayce on Channeling Your Higher Self. Warner Books, N.Y. 1989.

Sogyal, Rinpoche. The Tibetan Book of Living & Dying. Harper. San Francisco. 1994.

Sparrow, Lynn. Reincarnation, Claiming Your Past, Creating Your Future. St. Martin's Paperbacks. 1988.

Steiner, Rudolf. How To Know Higher Worlds. Anthroposophic Press. 1994.

Talbot, Michael. The Holographic Universe. Harper Collins Pub. N.Y. 1991.

Tanner, Wilma B. The Mystical, Magical, Marvelous World of Dreams. Sparrow Hawk Press. Tahlequah, OK. 1988.

Todeschi, Kevin. Edgar Cayce On the Akashic Records. A.R.E.Press. Va. Beach. 1998.

Trott, Susan. The Holy Man. Riverhead Books. N.Y. 1995.

Weiss, Brian. Through Time Into Healing. Simon & Schuster. N.Y. 1992.

White, John, ed. The Highest State of Consciousness. Anchor Books, N.Y. 1972.

Whitton, Joel, M.D., Fisher, Joe, Ph.D. Life Between Life. Warner Books, N.Y. 1986.

Wilber, Ken. Grace and Grit. Shambhala Pub. Boston. 1991.

------ One Taste: The Journals of Ken Wilber. Shambhala Pub. Boston. 1999.

About the Author

Professor Emeritus Marilyn Stacy is a psychotherapist in Dallas, Texas. She is married, has five grown children, two granddaughters, and five great-grandchildren. In addition to her private practice, she works with the non-profit, *Helping Our Helpers*. Marilyn has published articles, short stories, poems, and co-authored a college Psychology Applications text.

She began her book about out-of-body and other extra-sensory experiences several years ago, but set it aside, feeling the time was not right. This is her story of what is possible when disbelief is erased and doubts are set aside.

Lightning Source UK Ltd.
Milton Keynes UK
UKHW03f1607250318
319995UK00001B/49/P